Gender Confirmation Surgery

of related interest

Top to Bottom
A Memoir and Personal Guide Through Phalloplasty
Finlay Games
ISBN 978 1 78775 587 1
eISBN 978 1 78775 588 8

Trans Sex
A Guide for Adults
Kelvin Sparks
ISBN 978 1 83997 043 6
eISBN 978 1 83997 044 3

The Queer Mental Health Workbook
A Creative Self-Help Guide Using CBT, CFT and DBT
Dr Brendan J Dunlop
ISBN 978 1 83997 107 5
eISBN 978 1 83997 108 2

GENDER CONFIRMATION SURGERY

A GUIDE FOR TRANS AND NON-BINARY PEOPLE

EDWARD WHELAN

Illustrated by Nicholai Avigdor Melamed

Jessica Kingsley Publishers
London and Philadelphia

First published in Great Britain in 2023 by Jessica Kingsley Publishers
An imprint of John Murray Press

1

This book is intended to convey information to the reader. It is not intended
for medical diagnosis or treatment. The reader should seek appropriate
professional care and attention for any specific healthcare needs.

Content warning: This book mentions hospitalisation
and contains descriptions of surgery.

A CIP catalogue record for this title is available from the
British Library and the Library of Congress

ISBN 978 1 83997 096 2
eISBN 978 1 83997 097 9

Printed and bound in Great Britain by TJ Books Limited

Jessica Kingsley Publishers' policy is to use papers that are natural,
renewable and recyclable products and made from wood grown in
sustainable forests. The logging and manufacturing processes are expected
to conform to the environmental regulations of the country of origin.

Jessica Kingsley Publishers
Carmelite House
50 Victoria Embankment
London EC4Y 0DZ

www.jkp.com

John Murray Press
Part of Hodder & Stoughton Ltd
An Hachette Company

MIX
Paper from
responsible sources
FSC
www.fsc.org   FSC® C013056

Contents

1

The Basics

What this book is about

This book is for trans and non-binary people who are thinking about having a gender confirmation surgery. Gender confirmation surgery is an option for anyone transitioning gender. Transitioning can involve many steps:

- coming out
- changing your name
- taking hormones
- applying for a new passport or driving licence
- finding new clothes to wear, and more.

For some people, gender confirmation surgeries are also a part of the transitioning process.

Gender confirmation surgery is a choice for some trans and non-binary people, but it is not for everyone. It's important to make clear right away: gender confirmation surgery does not make you more or less trans, or more or less male, female or non-binary. It's just an option to consider. There are a whole range of gender confirmation surgeries to choose from. It's up to you to decide if any are right for you.

This book has information to introduce you to the different surgeries. It covers what changes each surgery aims to create, how the surgery is performed, who is eligible for the surgery, alternatives to surgery, common risks and complications to be aware of, tips on preparing for surgery and information on

GENDER CONFIRMATION SURGERY

recovering. There is also a chapter on scars and how to look after your skin after surgery. This book is a general guide, but all people are unique. Different bodies will change and heal in ways specific to them.

You can also find information on having a general anaesthetic, and why surgeons often require people to be below a certain weight or give up smoking to perform surgery.

This book also talks about how surgery affects when and how you can have children in the future and options around conceiving children, including pregnancy, in the chapter on fertility.

Gender confirmation surgery is not about sex, but it can have an impact on your sex life. The chapter on sex covers sex before surgery, and how transitioning can affect sexual behaviour.

There is also a chapter on sexual health and check-ups to understand your sexual health after surgery, and how transitioning might change which health check-ups you need.

While writing this book, I spoke with a group of trans and non-binary people about their experiences. Some of them chose surgery, some didn't. We talked about their decisions, how they feel about their bodies, what it was like going through surgery and recovering, how it impacted on their sexual behaviour and their thoughts about having children. You can find their stories at the end of the chapters on different surgeries.

The aim of this book is to give you enough information to understand your options. But it is not a replacement for speaking to surgeons.

And don't forget: you're allowed to change your mind. Whether you never thought you wanted surgery and now you do, you always wanted it and now you're not sure, or something else. The important thing that surgeons and trans and non-binary people all stress is to take your time and know your options.

I think being transgender is an incredibly strange thing in many ways. I think most of us are quite philosophical and struggle with it.

Maya

A short guide to trans and non-binary people

You might know loads about gender dysphoria and the transgender and non-binary spectrum, or you might know very little. So here are some key concepts.

The language around gender identity is changing all the time and there can be inconsistencies in how different people use it. Changes in language can be confusing, but gender identity beyond just male and female is an evolving area of understanding, and so the language reflects that.

What is gender and gender identity?

Gender refers to the socially constructed ideas of what is "masculine" and "feminine", such as how a masculine person should dress, how they should behave and what activities they should and shouldn't enjoy. Gender also covers what shape of body a masculine or feminine person should have, including what genitals they have. What is considered masculine or feminine varies across the world in different cultures and communities, and it has changed a lot throughout history.

Gender identity refers to our own sense of what our gender is. Our gender identity is a fundamental part of who we are.

Everyone is assigned a sex at birth, based on whether they are born with a penis or a vulva. At birth, these are the only parts of your body that look different for boys and girls. But a person's gender is not always the same as the sex they are assigned. Because of this, we know that gender isn't found in the genitals, or in the sex chromosomes that play a role in the body developing with a penis or a vulva.

There are quite a few different theories of gender identity. Studies have found biological, genetic, psychological and socio-cultural factors may all play a role in why some people are transgender. But there is still a lot that is unknown.

There is more to gender identity than just male and female. While some people identify as male or female, some people identify as somewhere in between, as both, or as neither. Gender identity is best thought of as a spectrum, a range of experiences, and each person's experience of their own gender will be unique to them.

We know that a gender identity that is different to the sex assigned at birth is not a delusion because it cannot be changed by psychiatric help. People are sometimes forced or choose to use conversion "therapy" to stop being transgender. But this is not a real form of therapy. Conversion "therapy" uses bullying, threats and violence.

Gender identity can be thought of as a bit like sexual orientation. It is fundamental to a person's self, but it cannot be identified with a microscope.

What is being transgender?

Transgender, or trans, is an umbrella term for a range of identities. It covers anyone who does not identify with the sex they were assigned at birth. This could be all or just some of the time. It could be a strong, deep feeling or a vague, lighter feeling.

There are a lot of different terms that can come under the "trans" umbrella: transsexual, female to male, male to female, non-binary, genderqueer, agender and others.

Not everyone who might be thought of as transgender uses the term. Some people might use the term before they transition and afterwards just refer to themselves as a woman or a man.

It is not known exactly how common being transgender is. Different studies have come up with very different figures. A study from 2015 estimated it at around 7 per 100,000 people.[1] Another study from around the same time estimated 871 per 100,000 people.[2] It has been found that the number of people experiencing gender dysphoria is increasing. But it is not known whether this is because the experience is becoming more widely known and spoken about or because the number is genuinely increasing.

---

1 Holmberg, M., Arver, S. and Dhejne, C. (2019). Supporting sexuality and improving sexual function in transgender persons. *Nature Reviews Urology*, *16*, 121–139. https://doi.org/10.1038/s41585-018-0108-8

2 Holmberg, M., Arver, S. and Dhejne, C. (2019). Supporting sexuality and improving sexual function in transgender persons. *Nature Reviews Urology*, *16*, 121–139. https://doi.org/10.1038/s41585-018-0108-8

Transgender and non-binary people's experiences around the world are hugely varied. Only some countries provide access to medical support for transitioning and legal recognition of transition.

What is being non-binary?

Non-binary is also an umbrella term for a range of identities people have that fall outside of male or female. They may be neither male nor female, or be both, at different times. Or they may have no feeling of gender at all.

Non-binary people may use the pronouns "they" rather than "she" or "he", and they may pick a gender-neutral name.

What is gender dysphoria?

When gender identity isn't aligned with your body, it can cause psychological distress. This is known as gender dysphoria.

How much gender dysphoria someone experiences can vary a great deal. For some it can be overwhelmingly unbearable; for others it is difficult but manageable. Some people find the dysphoria is focused on some parts of their body more than others.

Some people begin to talk about their gender dysphoria from a young age, while others come to understand their feelings of gender dysphoria later in life. All these experiences are valid.

Gender dysphoria is not related to sexual orientation. Someone with gender dysphoria may be gay, lesbian, bi, heterosexual or asexual.

Our understanding of sex and gender has not been concluded. Humans all over the world will continue to bring new nuance to the understanding of gender and our bodies.

Transitioning

Transitioning is the process many trans and non-binary people do to live in the gender they identify as. This can involve many different steps, and not everyone wants to do or can do all the steps. Some trans and non-binary people make very few changes to their lives and are happy. Others may want to make a lot of changes but find it difficult. They may not be able to afford the medical or administrative processes they want. They might not have the social support they need, either from their families, friends or at work. There may be legal barriers; for example, only around 15 countries allow people to have a gender-neutral passport.

Transitioning is sometimes separated into social transitioning and medical transitioning. Social transitioning includes steps such as:

- coming out to your friends and family
- coming out at work
- changing your name, and telling people your new name
- changing your pronouns, and telling everyone your new pronouns
- applying for a new passport and driving licence in your new name and gender
- changing your details with all your bills and accounts, such as gas, electric, phone, internet provider, bank, and changing your email if it included your name
- applying for new professional certificates to be created in your name
- changing how you dress and how you wear your hair
- changing your body language to something that feels more like yourself
- in some countries, applying for a new birth certificate.

Medical transitioning includes steps such as:

- taking hormones
- having electrolysis to permanently remove facial hair
- having surgery on your face or your upper or lower body.

These are not steps to become a different gender. All these changes are steps people take to live as the gender they are, to feel comfortable in their skin and be seen as the gender they are.

Who can have gender confirmation surgery?

Who is eligible for gender confirmation surgery is partly determined by a set of guidelines called the WPATH Standards of Care. These are guidelines created by the World Professional Association for Transgender Health. Many countries, including the UK and the USA, use these guidelines as the foundation for their own decisions on when people can begin a medical transition, including gender confirmation surgery.

Individual countries sometimes have their own additional guidelines. And specialist surgeons, such as craniofacial surgeons who work on facial feminisation surgery, may follow their own specialist guidelines too.

The WPATH Standards of Care are only guidelines, and they emphasise that each patient's individual preferences should always be taken into account.

Important note about the WPATH Standards of Care, version 8

In September 2022, a new version of the WPATH Standards of Care was published, version 8. This version has new guidance on who can have which surgeries, what age you need to be, what paperwork you need and more.

Below there is information about who is eligible for surgery based on the new standards. However, as they are very new, not everyone will know the details. Version 7 has been used since 2011, so you may find medical professionals still referring to the old standards.

The new standards are freely available for anyone to read on the WPATH website. If you think you have been asked to do something that isn't required, or you are unsure of your rights, you can refer to the Standards of Care or contact a transgender and non-binary advocacy organisation for advice.

Assessment and referral to surgery

The recommendations in the WPATH Standards of Care are for both the experience gender identity professionals should have and the criteria people need to meet before they can access medical treatment.

Adolescents

Adolescents wanting gender confirmation medical or surgical treatment first need to have a comprehensive physical and psychological assessment. WPATH recommends parents and guardians are involved in the assessment and treatment of adolescents, unless this would be harmful to the patient. Then, to access gender confirmation surgery, you need to meet all the following requirements:

- If a diagnosis is necessary to access healthcare, for example for health insurance, you meet the diagnostic criteria of gender incongruence in the *International Classification of Diseases* (ICD-11).
- Your experience of gender diversity or gender incongruence is marked and sustained over time.
- You can demonstrate the emotional and cognitive maturity required to give informed consent or assent for the treatment.[3]
- Any mental health concerns you have that could interfere with the diagnosis, your capacity to consent or the gender-affirming treatment have been addressed.
- You should have been told about any impact surgery will have on your fertility and your ability to have children. You should be informed of the options to preserve fertility.
- If you are choosing to take hormones, you should have had at least twelve months of hormone therapy before having surgery. This is only necessary for surgeries where hormones improve the surgical outcome.

---

3   Consent and assent are slightly different. To give consent you must be legally an adult, whereas you can assent to treatment as an adolescent.

Adults

For adults wanting gender conformation surgery, you need to meet the following criteria:

- Your experience of gender incongruence is marked and has been sustained over time.
- If a diagnosis is necessary to access healthcare, for example for health insurance, you meet the diagnostic criteria of gender incongruence in the International Classification of Diseases (ICD-11).
- Other possible causes for gender incongruence have been evaluated.
- Any physical or mental health conditions that could negatively impact the outcome of your gender-affirming treatment have been assessed. The risks and benefits of the treatment have been discussed with you.
- You have the capacity to consent to the surgery.
- You understand the effect of gender-affirming treatment on reproduction and have explored reproductive options, if wanted, before beginning treatment.
- If you are taking hormones, you are stable on the regime.
- For surgeries where hormones can improve the outcome, six months on hormones before surgery is recommended. This is only for people who are choosing to take hormones.

To be clear: being on hormones is not a requirement for having surgery for either adults or adolescents. But if you are taking them, they recommend being on hormones for twelve months (for adolescents) and six months (for adults) before having surgery, except for hysterectomy and chest reconstruction.

Being on hormones for a period of time can potentially improve the outcome of the surgery. For example, breast augmentation results can improve if the breast tissue has had time to develop from taking hormones. Metoidioplasty benefits from the clitoris growth you get from hormones. And for orchiectomy, the WPATH Standards of Care recommend people experience the hormonal changes they will feel after surgery beforehand, by suppressing testosterone.

However, the WPATH Standards of Care also state that facial and chest surgery before hormones can help social transition.

Once you meet these criteria, adults and adolescents both need just one opinion or referral letter from a professional experienced in assessing transgender and gender diverse people for gender confirmation surgery. Your surgeon will probably need to see this letter before taking you on as a patient.

Diagnosis

The ICD-11 is a manual that lists diseases and illnesses, including "gender incongruence". In many countries, including the USA, a diagnosis is required in order to access healthcare, for example, for insurers to contribute. You can read the ICD-11 online. In the UK, the NHS requires a diagnosis of "gender dysphoria" before creating a treatment plan. Gender dysphoria is listed in the Diagnostic and Statistical Manual, 5th edition (DSM-5), a list of illnesses and disorders used in the UK.

The language in this book

It is difficult to talk about the changes that gender confirmation surgery achieves without using terms like "masculine" and "feminine", or "male" and "female".

People transition for personal reasons. The reasons may include a mix of changing your body to feel better in your own skin and also so other people see you as you want to be seen. Knowing yourself to be, for example, female, is not enough for many trans people; we need to be seen as female.

Therefore, we describe the surgeries in this book as moving people towards being *seen* as female or male, rather than *being* female or male. The difference is important. Your gender is not in your face, your chest or your genitals, but it is seen there. So when a trans man has chest reconstruction, we describe it as creating a chest that is seen as male.

This book covers surgery to parts of the body, such as the chest or genitals, which can be difficult to read about if they trigger feelings of gender dysphoria. We know people sometimes find it easier to refer to these parts of the body with slang terms. But in order to avoid confusion, we will be using the anatomical names for parts of the body throughout the book. In each chapter, there are diagrams of bodies to introduce you to terms you might not be familiar with.

In the stories at the end of each chapter, some people talk about "passing" or "being passable". Passing refers to being seen by other people as the gender you are. It is not a term everybody likes to use, because it could suggest that passing is a trick – that you are "passing as male", for example, rather than "being male". But this is not how everyone uses the term, and for some people it just means being seen as the gender they are.

How this book was written

Getting information from reliable sources is important, so I want to be clear about how I wrote this book. I am not a doctor or a medical professional. All the information in this book was gathered from trustworthy sources such as peer-reviewed journals, websites such as NHS.uk or from professional organisations such as BAPRAS. You can find the full list of the sources of information at the end of the book, and many are free to access online.

2

Thinking about Surgery

Whether you are certain about the surgery you want or only just starting to think about your options, it's essential to be clear about what you are hoping to achieve, both physically and psychologically. You are more likely to be happy with the result if you had realistic expectations going in.

Setting realistic expectations
Realistic expectations: How it will look
Look at "before and after" photos to get a sense of the range of results from the surgery you are interested in. You can find collections of surgical results online, such as on transbucket.com. Also, many trans and non-binary bloggers share their results on their social media channels, such as YouTube, Instagram or TikTok. At a consultation, the surgeon should also offer you before and after photos of surgeries they have performed.

Look at results from people who went to different surgeons, who have different body shapes and are different ages. Everyone's body is different, and how one person's surgery turned out does not mean it will be the same for you.

There are lots of places to find before and after images of surgery, but be sure to look at results both in the first months after surgery and how things will look four or five years later. Surgery results can look bruised, scabbed, swollen and a bit gross at first.

Some of the scars from surgeries in this book take a year or more to fade and for the body to look more like how it will long term.

Realistic expectations: How long the whole process takes

Going through one or several gender confirmation surgeries can take a long time. For each surgery, consider creating a timeline for each of the steps you need to take and map in any other events happening in your life, at home or at work, as you go. There are other things to take into account other than just the recovery time from the surgery itself.

Depending on which surgery you are thinking about, plot in time to:

- be on a waiting list
- lose a little weight, if your surgeon recommends it (see Chapter 12: Preparing for Surgery)
- need revisions or follow-up surgery
- have procedures in preparation, such as hair removal or a hysterectomy
- arrange options for future fertility, such as freezing sperm or eggs
- look after your mental health, and get to a place where you are stable and have support around you if you need it
- take a break between surgeries. After recovery, your body will need some time off before you can have the next surgery
- avoid immovable work or life events, such as exams.

Of course, some things you can't plan for and won't know in advance when they will happen. But lots of the steps you can know in advance and give yourself time to do them.

Realistic expectations: Information from a range of sources

It's important to gather accurate information and good advice. There are a lot of different kinds of information available online about gender confirmation surgery. Different types of information have different uses. Personal stories are useful, but they don't always represent the average experience. Surgeons' websites are helpful, but they may be selling their services and over-represent their success. Medical journals and textbooks are helpful but can focus on the details of the surgery and not how it feels afterwards. Talking to people online is helpful, but there is often no way to check whether their good or bad experiences are true. So be choosy about where you find information and consider how useful each kind is.

Reading about different surgical options can bring up a lot of questions. Keep a note somewhere of the questions you have. There is space at the back of the book to jot down questions as they come up.

I went to a group called PFLAG; that's where I learnt a lot of things, and where I got my start in finding resources. I was able to meet a bunch of different trans individuals of different identities. I became very close to a trans woman who was in her 60s going through transition and had surgery the following year after I met her. She was kind of a big sister, somebody who helped me along, who helped give me resources and support.

Mikey

Realistic expectations: Understand the risks

When you read about different surgical procedures and speak with doctors, you will probably hear about different amounts of risk. Something might be described as a "common" risk for example, or a "rare" risk.

All surgery comes with a risk of complications. But some complications have a higher risk than others, and some complications are worse than others, whether they're more or less likely to happen. Surgery also comes with benefits, so when looking at surgical options, weigh up the risks with the benefits. There can be uncertainty around risk, and you may hear different information from different medical practitioners.

There is never zero risk, but what you consider worth the risk is individual to you.

When a doctor is discussing risk with you, they will give you numbers based on the chance of something happening in the entire population. For example, one in eight women develop breast cancer. But this statistic cannot tell you if you will be the one. The doctor might also describe something as "rare" or "uncommon". Medical practitioners in the UK and Europe are expected to use a common language for talking about risk:

Verbal description	Risk	Risk description
Very common	1 in 1 to 1 in 10	A person in family
Common	1 in 10 to 1 in 100	A person in street
Uncommon	1 in 100 to 1 in 1000	A person in village
Rare	1 in 1000 to 1 in 10,000	A person in small town
Very rare	Less than 1 in 10,000	A person in large town

When you are reading about risk, it can be easy to be misled depending on how the information is presented. For example, if a risk is said to be double for people over a certain age, this can sound like a lot. But a risk doubling could mean it had changed from 1 in 6000 to 1 in 3000 (the same as 2 in 6000). You can see from the table above that the risk would still be "rare".

When discussing risk with a doctor, consider the following:

- What are the chances of this complication occurring?
- How much harm can it do, if it occurs?
- Is the harm permanent or can it be fixed, if it occurs?
- Is there anything about your own circumstances, your age or health, that changes the risk?
- You can also ask for them to explain numbers in different ways, or ask for them to be repeated.

Realistic expectations: Keep looking after your mental health

Gender confirmation surgery can relieve gender dysphoria and lead to a boost in your general mental health. But mental health problems can stem from different places, and some issues take a long time to resolve. Some people with certain mental health problems are advised to take medication long term. Do not stop taking medication without speaking to your doctor.

And while surgery can give your confidence a boost and relieve gender dysphoria, it can also be a stressful and frustrating process to go through. Sometimes surgery doesn't go perfectly the first time and you need a second to fix a complication.

Realistic expectations: Body image is important

Having surgery can improve confidence in your body. But it can be hard to know before surgery the difference between feelings of gender dysphoria and other body image problems. Gender confirmation surgery may not relieve all the discomfort you have with your body. Aim to have a realistic idea for what surgery can do, and what it can't.

It is helpful for family and friends, and anyone supporting you, to also have realistic expectations of what the surgery can and can't achieve, the common complications and the recovery time.

An exercise to help you think through the surgery

Choosing whether to have surgery or not, as well as which surgery is right for you, can be fraught with emotional pressures. These could be pressure from friends or partners to have surgery or to not have any. Or you might be weighing up whether the cost and the risk of complications are worth it. Every gender confirmation surgery has pros and cons to compare.

It is easy to fixate on getting surgery and not think about the downsides. Try using the following table to help untangle your thoughts and feelings for each surgery you're considering, to help see if it might be right for you. Use the table how you want; there aren't right or wrong answers.

A part of your body you'd like to change: . . . .

. . . .

A surgery you are thinking of having: . . . .

. . . .

	Physically	Emotionally	Socially
How does this part of my body currently bother me?			
What are my goals for this part?			
What will surgery change?			
What will surgery not change?			
What are the risks with having surgery?			
Your own question:			

The Five Cs[1]

As you read through this book, keep in mind the Five Cs.

1. Think about the **change** you want to see, and what you think it will do for your life. Be open to your wishes not being achievable. Be aware of the limitations of surgery and how much it can change you. Listen to yourself. There are a range of options available. But what is important is to know what, if anything, is right for you.

2. **Check out** potential surgeons. Ensure they are registered with organisations where you can verify their qualifications. Don't rush into a decision using a time-limited offer. Ensure they make you feel comfortable. They should have experience working with trans and non-binary clients. If something isn't right, pause.

3. Have a **consultation** with the surgeon who will do your surgery. Have a second consultation if you are still unsure or have more questions. Bring prepared questions – there are examples in each chapter, and you can use the Notes section at the end of this book to jot these down ahead of time. Be honest with your surgeon, and clear about what you want and why. You should leave the consultation clear about the whole process.

4. Get the **cash** together. Whether you are paying for the surgery yourself, have medical insurance or are covered by your country's medical care, there are likely still going to be things you have to pay for.
   - Some surgeries require preparation such as electrolysis.
   - You will need time off work to recover.
   - You may need extra prescriptions.
   - There could be long travel to appointments.
   - You might need to stay overnight in a hotel if your surgery is a long way home.

---

1   The Five Cs are inspired by the BAPRAS campaign Think Over Before You Make Over. See www.bapras.org.uk/public/patient-information/think-over-before-you-make-over.

- If you bring someone with you for support, they may need to travel and stay overnight.
- Sometimes surgery has complications, and this could mean more travel back and forth to a hospital.
- Some surgical procedures don't last a lifetime, and you may need revisions as you age.
- Consider preparing a budget for the costs of going through surgery ahead of time.

5. **Care** about your aftercare. If any complications do occur, you will need to be able to get to the clinic or hospital. When you leave the hospital, be clear about who to contact for what problems. You may need a visiting nurse or to go for a wound check. Be sure you have a list of the next steps. How well you take care of yourself after surgery can be just as important as the surgery itself. All surgery takes a toll on your body, and you need to rest to let it heal, even if you're not in pain or if the surgical incisions are very small.

MAYA'S STORY

Maya looked into facial surgery for a few years before deciding not to have any. She is now considering lower surgery and talked to me about the different factors she weighed up while thinking through her options.

I started looking into facial feminisation surgery by speaking to a few different surgeons and going to conferences. My goal was always to try to do things as naturally as possible. Even though I felt 100 per cent correct in what I was doing, I wanted to understand myself before I made any changes.

But when I looked into facial feminisation surgery, at the results and the techniques used, there were a few things that worried me. The radicalness of the surgeries, and the risks associated with them. I wanted to know, should something go wrong, after you've parted with your money, what sort of response would you have to fix things?

I really wanted to "pass", so that gave me a strong desire

for surgery. But I was still early in my journey. I wanted time to accept myself and my identity as it was emerging, before I started playing with it. I was trying to teach myself to be patient; knowing I'd only been on hormones a short amount of time, there were still changes that would take place. And I was trying to see if I could get comfortable if I had some masculine features. I was looking at pictures of film stars who shared some characteristics to my face, to understand them. How do they dress themselves, what make up do they use, how do they enhance themselves?

One of the things that helped me was the Reclaim Pride march. I was trying to make myself as "passable" as possible when I suddenly thought, *No, this is about pride in who you are, you need to just embrace that you're a transgender woman and that's okay.* I think being transgender is an incredibly strange thing in many ways. I think most of us are quite philosophical and struggle with it.

I had a lot of questions but also felt if there's something surgical that's borderline whether you need it or not, I think it's best to not do anything. For me, I don't want to look overly beautiful, and I don't want a surgeon trying to sell me their perception of beautiful. I just want to be female without being challenged.

I got to a place where I was comfortable choosing not to have facial surgery, and then I started thinking about lower surgery. There's always been a profound misalignment between my body and how my mind sees me. Hormones have changed my body; my testicles are smaller and a lot of the time they are internal, and the way I orgasm is different as well. So I do feel like I'm in a new body, though it's not quite where I need it to be. Recently I was invited to a hammam, which is like a steam room in a Turkish bath. I wore some bikini bottoms, but I still felt that distance away from where I'd like to be.

And there is the question of physical intimacy. I'm still with my partner since before I transitioned; we've been together for about thirty years, but we haven't had sex for around ten years or so. We just kind of drifted. Part of that, though, was because I wasn't comfortable. I was interested in sex, but I just wasn't comfortable. And my partner is not interested in female bodies. But I need to have that intimacy in my life, and I would like to be intimate as female.

But then, I think, I overcame the initial need to get facial surgery, so that could also happen for the rest of my body. There's a lot of convenience with having a male body. I do a lot of sports, and being able to pee standing up is handy. And I'm a cyclist, so being comfortable in the saddle genuinely concerns me; I don't want to suddenly lose the ability to cycle because of surgery. And then there are huge risks to lower surgery; there's a lot of dedication involved and complications to go through. I am pretty lucky: I was born in a healthy body, albeit the wrong gender. But other than that, I'm looking at major surgery on a healthy body, so I ask myself – can I learn to live with my body with where it's at? I think surgery could be a way of disconnecting from the old me. I want to be careful I'm not doing it just to get away from the past. I have to do it 100 per cent for me.

3

Breast Augmentation

Breast augmentation surgery puts an implant inside the chest to make the breast bigger. You might want larger breasts to feel more comfortable in your body, to be seen more often as a woman or if your breasts are different sizes and you want a symmetrical shape.

The effect of hormone therapy on breast growth

As a child, everyone's breasts are the same. Then at puberty, oestrogen causes the breasts to grow. Everyone produces oestrogen at puberty. But if your body is also producing testosterone at the same time, the testosterone prevents the breasts from growing.

Taking oestrogen as hormone therapy can cause your body fat to move to your hips, bum and breasts.

However, taking oestrogen often leads to only a small amount of breast growth. One study found almost half the participants had a cup size of AAA after a year of taking oestrogen and anti-androgens.[1] Most of the growth in breast size happens in the first six months of hormone therapy and stops after about two years. This is the same even if you gain weight or increase the level of oestrogen in your blood.

Some people are also prescribed progestin as part of their hormone therapy. Progestin is a form of another hormone,

---

1   de Blok, C.J.M., *et al.* (2018). Breast development in transwomen after 1 year of cross-sex hormone therapy: results of a prospective multicenter study. *The Journal of Clinical Endocrinology & Metabolism, 103*(2), 532–538. https://doi.org/10.1210/jc.2017-01927

progesterone. There is not strong evidence that progestin can improve breast development. The WPATH Standards of Care note that some clinicians believe that progestin is necessary for breast growth, but this has not been found to be the case.

How the surgery is performed

Breast augmentation usually involves an incision in the crease under the breast, and the implant is placed either between the skin and the muscle or under the muscle. Sometimes the incision will be made in the armpit (a transaxillary incision) or around the nipple (a peri-areolar incision).

Placing the breast implant

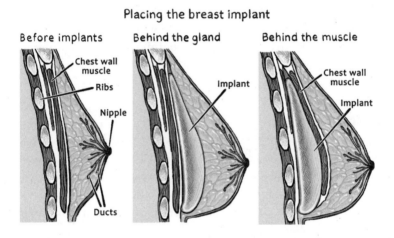

The advantage of the armpit method is it hides the incision very well; however, it is only suitable for saline or very small silicone implants because of the small size of the incision. Saline implants are inserted empty and then filled with saline once they are in place. The "around the nipple" method can also hide the incision well because of the darker skin of the nipple. However, if the scar doesn't heal well, it is more visible, and with this type of incision there is a risk of damaging nerves in the nipples, resulting in a loss of sensation.

The method of placing the implant behind the muscle is

suitable for people with very little chest tissue or whose ribs are visible through the skin. The muscle adds more padding around the implant and avoids the edge of the implant being noticeable. Lipofilling can also hide the edges of the implant. Lipofilling involves removing a small amount of fat from one part of your body (such as the thighs or stomach) and injecting it around the breasts to cover the edges of the implant.

Because their bodies produced testosterone during puberty, trans women and non-binary people assigned male at birth often have broad shoulders and wide chests. This can make it difficult to create cleavage. Surgeons aim to insert breast implants in line with where the nipple sits, so the nipple sits on the largest point – the tip of the mound of the implant – which looks most natural. If the implants sat closer together, creating more cleavage, the nipples would be off centre. It is possible to move the nipples in a procedure known as a mastopexy, but this can lead to numbness in the nipples.

Size and shape

Breast implants are measured in weight or millilitres. At the consultation, the surgeon will be able to advise you on the sizes suitable for your body, but they can't guarantee a cup size. Most people will have a range of sizes of implants that would be suitable for them, and you can choose whether you want to be at the larger or smaller end.

Silicone implants can come in different shapes: round or teardrop. Teardrop silicone implants are sometimes called anatomical, as they are thought to look more natural, with more of the volume at the base. But one review found no aesthetic advantage of the teardrop shape, and surgeons could not identify the different shapes once they had been implanted.

There are a number of different brands of breast implants, but they are all either filled with silicone or saline. There are two different types of silicone that can be used. Some brands use a thick liquid gel and others use a firmer gel, sometimes called a "gummy bear" implant, because of how it can retain its shape if damaged. The outer of all implants is silicone, though some have an extra polyurethane layer on the outside.

Your surgeon should also talk to you about the profile of different implants. The profile is the combination of how wide the flat base of the implant is – that lies against your body – and how far out from your body it projects. Implants of the same weight can have different profiles. A "low" profile implant has a wide base and the least projection, whereas an "ultra-high profile" implant has a very narrow base and projects the furthest from the body. Middle-range profiles look most natural. Teardrop-shaped implants are measured in width and projection, but also in height. So there is a wide range of different shapes and sizes to try.

Alternatives to breast implants

If you are too young for surgery, on a long waiting list or saving up the cost, there are still a few ways you can change your body proportions. There is a variety of lingerie and accessories that are designed to change your shape by making your breasts appear bigger, increasing your cleavage or cinching your waist. These accessories are used by cisgender people and trans people.

Bra inserts

Inserts can be added into your bra to give your breasts more size. They are reusable and available from many different shops. They are usually made from lightweight foam or gel and sit in your bra in front of your breast. They can be found in different skin tones as well as transparent and sometimes come with an outline of a nipple for a realistic shape against thin material. They might also be called "breast forms" (some people also call them "chicken fillets", as they are a similar shape). You can also buy "cleavage boosters" that don't increase breast size so much as push the breasts together to create more cleavage.

Padded bras

Padded bras are exactly what they sound like: bras with added padding to give breasts more size and shape under clothing.

They are widely available, and you can also get swimsuits with a padded breast area.

Padded bras are slightly different from push-up bras. A push-up bra is designed to increase the size of your cleavage by pushing the breasts together, whereas a padded bra gives the whole breast a larger shape.

There are other ways you can change the proportions of your torso. You can cinch your waist with shapewear, waist cinchers or lightweight corsets. These are often available in lingerie departments or from online specialists. You can also buy padding for the hips and bum. The disadvantage of these, though, is they can be hot to wear under clothing.

Lipofilling

As mentioned, lipofilling is sometimes used alongside implants, but it can also be used as an alternative to them. Lipofilling on its own is suitable when you want a small increase in the size of your breasts, or to even out the shape or symmetry of your breasts. Fat from another part of your body is extracted with a needle, cleaned and then injected around the breasts.

Only your own fat can be used for lipofilling; all other materials that have been used in the past have been proven to be unsafe.

Complications that can occur with breast implants

As with all surgery, there is a risk of bleeding and infection. There are also some risks to be aware of that are particular to breast augmentation surgery.

Changes to nipple sensation

Nipples can become numb or overly sensitive. This might be temporary or permanent.

Implants moving and changing shape

Breast implants can change shape over time, just like natural breasts do. An implant can also sometimes rotate, most often during sleep. It will usually adjust itself or can be pushed back into shape.

Capsular contracture

When an implant is placed into the body, the body will form a scar around it. This is called the capsule. In some patients, the capsule contracts, which can make the breast feel harder. Sometimes this does not change the overall look of the breast and no further surgery is needed. But sometimes the hardness can change the shape of the breast, make it more rounded, and it can make it tender. If this happens, speak to your doctor to consider your options. You may need to have an operation to replace the implant.

The risk of "noticeable firmness" or capsular contracture is one in ten of all implants, but most don't need replacing. When someone has experienced capsular contracture, the chance of it happening again when the implant is replaced is one in two.

BIA-ALCL (breast implant associated anaplastic large cell lymphoma)

There is an association between breast implants and a rare form of cancer of the white blood cells. It's called breast implant associated anaplastic large cell lymphoma, or BIA-ALCL. Like other lymphomas, BIA-ALCL is a cancer of the immune system and not of breast tissue, so it isn't breast cancer.

In the UK, the majority of cases are cured by removing the implants and the scar tissue around them (the capsule). It is not currently known why some people develop BIA-ALCL and others do not.

The most common symptom is a painless build-up of fluid around the implant. You would notice the implant quickly getting larger, over the course of a few weeks. It might affect one or both implants. Less commonly a lump forms around the implant, or the capsule contracts.

There is no screening or tests for BIA-ALCL. If you have any of the symptoms, you should speak to your doctor, or contact the hospital where you had the implants put in and make an appointment to see the surgeon.

In general, if you have a problem with your breasts, or find any swelling, lumps or changes in shape, speak to your GP. If you think the implants themselves are causing you problems, make an appointment with the original hospital or clinic where you had the surgery.

Breast implants don't last a lifetime

Depending on the age at which you had the implants, you will probably need to have them replaced at least once during your lifetime. Implants are designed to be tough, but it is estimated that around half of them will become damaged within fifteen years of being put in. You don't have to replace implants at the point that they need to be removed, but the shape of your breasts could be sagged and wrinkled without the implant inside. It is important therefore to be financially prepared to replace the implants.

The implant gets damaged

If an implant gets damaged it may need to be replaced, for example, if it receives a strong impact from a car accident. Implants experience wear and tear over time and an older implant is more likely to become damaged.

If you have a saline implant, and the saline leaks, it can safely be reabsorbed into the body. If you have a silicone implant, small amounts of silicone can leak out. Most people do not react to the silicone, but sometimes it can cause inflammation around the leaked silicone, causing silicone granuloma.

If the implant ruptures and gel comes out, you may notice lumpiness around the breast. You will be advised to have the implant removed, and if you choose, replaced.

Around 1 in 100 people a year need to have revision surgery for their breast implants.[2]

The implant is visible

If you have very little body fat, and little breast tissue, there is a risk of the edges of the implant being visible beneath the skin. This can sometimes be improved with lipofilling. The ripples of

---

2   BAPRAS (2021). Your Guide to Breast Augmentation. www.bapras.org.
     uk/docs/default-source/default-document-library/print_bapras_breast_
     aug_2021-(final)-(revised)-(7).pdf?sfvrsn=0

the implant can sometimes also be seen through the skin, again often if you have low body fat. Saline implants are more likely to have visible ripples, but silicone ones can ripple too.

Choosing a surgeon

There are many different hospitals that offer breast augmentation surgery. Depending on the cost, you can meet with more than one surgeon if you choose, to find one that feels right.

You want to find a surgeon who has been trained in the specific surgery you are looking for, offers clear information about their services, gives examples of their work and has a good reputation working with trans and non-binary people. After you have found a surgical service you like, book a consultation.

There are different ways to check the experience and qualifications of the surgeon you are looking at, plus ways to check the reputation of the hospital or clinic they work for. Different countries have different organisations that keep an independent register of surgeons. In the UK, try looking up your doctor on the General Medical Council website. Or if you're visiting a hospital or clinic, you can look them up on the Care Quality Commission website. In the USA, try searching for your doctor on the Federation of State Medical Boards website.

Going for a consultation

A consultation is a chance to meet the surgeon who will perform your surgery and discuss your different options. They will take into account how firm your skin is, the size of your ribcage and how much breast tissue you already have. It's important you have a consultation with the surgeon and not just a representative from the hospital or clinic. A representative may not be able to answer in enough detail the questions you have about the surgery.

To help you consider different sizes and shapes, some surgeons may offer you implant sizers. These fit into your bra so you can get a sense of how the finished result will look. Other surgeons use 3D photography.

A consultation usually lasts between a half hour and an hour, and you will probably have to pay for it. Because the time is limited, it's a good idea to have your questions prepared in advance to make sure you get all the answers you want. Below is a list of suggested questions. There is space at the end of the book to write down more questions.

- What range of sizes and shapes is right for me?
- What are the differences between silicone and saline implants?
- Who is the implant manufacturer, and why do you use that brand?
- Should I have the implant under the chest muscle or just under the skin, or under both?
- I have a long-term health condition; how will it impact the surgery and my recovery?
- I take medication; how will that impact the surgery and my recovery?
- When can the surgery be scheduled? What if I need it rescheduled?
- How much does the surgery cost, and what does that cover? Do you take my health insurance?
- If there are complications and I need a second surgery, does the original payment cover that?
- How do you take payment, and is it possible to pay in instalments?
- How long will I be in hospital?
- How long should I take off work or study?
- How long have you been performing breast augmentation? How many procedures have you done?
- What qualifications do you have? What training do you have? Are you a member of a relevant professional association?
- Can I see photos of your recent work?
- Have you worked with trans and non-binary people previously?

- What complications can occur, and how likely are they?
- What will it look like straight out of surgery, and how will it change over time?
- What should I do if I am not happy with the result?
- What aftercare do you provide?
- When will I need the implants replaced, and how will I know that they need replacing?
- Do I need to do anything in preparation for surgery?

If you are paying for surgery, you should be offered a package price before the consultation. Avoid services that require you to pay for the whole procedure before the consultation, ask for non-refundable deposits or give offers or time-limited deals. The package price you are offered should cover any complications that arise. Keep in mind: the cheapest deal is probably not the best.

You should not feel rushed into surgery. Your surgeon should be able to offer you a range of sizes and materials for your implants and be able to discuss why they recommend them. Some surgeons offer a cooling-off period to give you time to think.

Before going into hospital and going into hospital

If you take hormone therapy, it is unlikely you will need to stop taking it before having breast augmentation. If you smoke or vape, though, you will probably need to stop smoking before the surgery and continue not to smoke afterwards.

The surgery itself takes around one to one and a half hours. You will probably spend one night in hospital, depending on how well you're recovering. Then, people are usually advised to take one to two weeks off work or study to ensure they can heal and recuperate.

While there will probably be some discomfort after surgery, the pain is usually easily managed with painkillers. You can expect to be back to full exercise (running, swimming, yoga) after around six weeks. But listen to your body, and follow your surgeon's advice.

Recovery

Immediately after the surgery, the implants may be sitting quite high, or they may look too high up or too round and not natural. It can take around three to four months for the implants to drop into their final positions.

When you are home from the hospital, you will probably find you are sore and have limited movement of your arms, particularly lifting your arms, so prepare your home in advance so everything you need is within easy reach.

If your surgeon recommends a surgical bra to be worn after your procedure, they can be bought from high street department stores. Remember that it will need to be a larger cup size. You will probably also need clothes that fasten at the front like shirts, blouses and zip-up tops, because putting clothes on over your head might be difficult or tug on your stitches.

Mammograms

There is no relationship between breast implants and breast cancer,[3] or cancer in any other part of the body other than the rare BIA-ALCL. However, if you have breast growth from taking oestrogen, it is important to regularly check for lumps in your breasts and go for a mammogram every three years.

Breast implants sit behind the breasts and push them forward, so they don't interfere with looking and feeling for lumps in your own body. The implants, though, can slightly reduce the efficacy of a mammogram.

Trans and non-binary people assigned male at birth who take oestrogen may have a slightly higher risk[4] of developing breast cancer than cisgender men (for cisgender men it is about 1 in 833

---

3   BAPRAS (2021). Your Guide to Breast Augmentation. www.bapras.org.uk/docs/default-source/default-document-library/print_bapras_breast_aug_2021-(final)-(revised)-(7).pdf?sfvrsn=0
4   Cancer Research UK (2023). I'm Trans or Non-binary, Does This Affect My Screening? www.cancerresearchuk.org/about-cancer/cancer-symptoms/spot-cancer-early/screening/trans-and-non-binary-cancer-screening#screening20

people[5]). But trans and non-binary people assigned male at birth who take oestrogen have a lower risk than cisgender women (for cisgender women the risk is 1 in 8[6]). There are also differences in risk depending on your ethnicity. Breast cancer is about 100 times less common among white men than among white women. But it is about 70 times less common among Black men than Black women.

It is also thought you are more at risk if you have a family history of breast cancer, if you have been taking oestrogen or progesterone for more than five years, if you are overweight or if you are 50 or older. Therefore, if you take hormone therapy it is important to go for regular mammograms.

Having a mammogram

A mammogram, also known as a breast screening, is a form of X ray. It is designed to detect small signs of breast cancer that are too small to see or feel. It is performed at a screening clinic or sometimes at a mobile unit.

At the mammogram you will be asked to undress down to your waist, including underwear. It is a good idea to wear trousers, a skirt or dungarees so it is easy to remove just the top half of your clothing. You will stand against a screening machine and it will press against your breasts.

Breast screenings can be uncomfortable or sometimes painful, as they involve the breasts being flattened. But the discomfort doesn't last long.

Depending on which country you live in, the recommendations vary slightly about how often you need a breast screening. In the UK, it is recommended that you get a mammogram every three years if you are aged between 50 and 71 years old. In the USA, the CDC recommends getting a mammogram every two years if you are aged 50 or over.

If you have breast implants, let the clinic know when you

5   American Cancer Society (2023). Key Statistics for Breast Cancer in Men. www.cancer.org/cancer/breast-cancer-in-men/about/key-statistics.html
6   NHS (2023). Breast Cancer in Women. www.nhs.uk/conditions/breast-cancer

make an appointment. You can still have a mammogram with breast implants, but you may be directed to a different clinic.

In the UK, if you are registered as female with your GP, you will get automatic letters every three years once you're over the age of 50 inviting you to a breast screening. Some GPs have gender options other than "male" and "female", but not all do.

If you are not registered with a GP, or not registered as female, or not within the age group, you can still have a breast screening. Contact your GP for a referral.

Final thing

Women's breasts come in all shapes and sizes, and some people have none at all. Take the time to find the right shape for the body you want.

MIKEY'S STORY

Mikey is 21 and lives in Maryland, USA. She had breast augmentation in 2021, and during the same surgery had vaginoplasty revisions.

I knew what I wanted. Ever since I was a little girl, I've always wanted decent-sized boobs, and hormones didn't really get me there. I had breast development, but if I was standing up it would be flat; it would fall into my body.

I thought I was going to get a B or a C cup, but I went from a flat chest to a 36DD, which is fairly big. But I love them.

I had breast augmentation in 2021 and also revisions on my vaginoplasty, during the same surgery. I'd had a few minor complications to my first vaginoplasty. The revisions helped open up the canal because it had tightened during recovery and it was harder to dilate. Plus the surgeon did a little bit of reconstruction on the labia majora to help fix where I'd torn my stitches. So they were all part of my breast augmentation surgery.

At the consultation, we looked at implants and tried some

implant sizers on. Sizers are bra inserts; one side is kind of a teardrop boob, and then the other side is just flat. You just place it on your chest and then put the bra over the top to see how the different sizes will look.

I could have had my choice of saline or silicone and I'm sure even if I'd asked for a certain brand I probably would have been able to get that. But I said to the surgeon – you work with these every day, you know what you're doing, you pick the material you are comfortable with, and what you think is best for me and my body.

So I got silicone implants. One is 325 cc and one is 350 cc, so just a little bit bigger. Just to make sure they look even.

The recovery wasn't as bad as I thought it was going to be. It really only took two weeks for me to heal, which was surprising; I was expecting it to be much longer. For the breast augmentation, I was completely fine within two days. If it was just that operation it would have been a piece of cake. You have to wear a really tight surgical bra for two weeks. There's a little bit of shortness of breath and tightness but that's really it.

I remember the first time I saw them. I was in my bathroom, my boyfriend was with me, and I unclipped the surgical bra and opened it up and they went *whoosh*. I was like, *Oh my god they're too big, what the heck?* But that's just because they hadn't softened up, they were still very firm, the implants were hard and the skin wasn't loose enough to make it look soft. They just barely fit in my body at first, so my skin was really tight.

For the first week or two, when I took a shower, I'd be holding on to them because it felt like the pressure of letting them go was just going to make them fall out. Even though I knew they weren't, that's what it felt like. It felt extremely weird.

But over time as the skin got used to the implants, they've softened up. I forget that I have them now because they're just so soft, it just feels so natural. They felt like part of me extremely quickly.

I had a very progressive health insurance that saw breast

augmentation as medically necessary. Trans people's faces and chests are seen by society, but not necessarily their genitals. So one could argue that facial surgery and top surgery are more medically necessary than bottom surgery,[7] because everybody sees your face and body.

I feel so much more confident having breasts. It's something I always envisioned for myself, as a woman. That is womanhood for me. They're a pain in the butt sometimes, but being able to have them has made me feel so much more me. When I'm in a bathing suit, or wearing a really pretty dress or top where cleavage shows, it makes me feel so good. I just feel confident in my skin because now everybody sees this part of me.

What I wish I'd known before surgery

Stretch marks! After I first got surgery, I had bright red stretch marks all around my nipples, and then they just kind of stretched out to my entire boobs so it felt like it's all stretch marks and I hated it. I was so upset about it for such a long time. But after a few months they are completely light and unnoticeable.

I'm like, you know what, whatever. I started scar treatment for the incision marks under my boobs and on my labia, but I stopped because I said – those are my battle wounds. Those are my battle scars. I don't need to look perfect. I wish I could, but I've become okay that I don't. I'm thankful that they're there to remind me where I came from. To remind me of the journey.

---

7 "Top surgery" means chest reconstruction or breast augmentation. "Bottom surgery" or "lower surgery" means any of the surgeries for the genitals.

4

Chest Reconstruction

Chest reconstruction aims to change the shape of the chest so it will be seen as male. For some people this is part of their transition to male; for others it is to achieve a "neutral look". There are several different surgical options, depending on the size of your chest and your preferences for the look and feel of the finished result. Chest reconstruction removes the need to wear a binder under your clothes to flatten your chest.

The main differences between the methods for chest reconstruction are where the scars are left, how big the scars are and whether you keep sensation in your nipples. But not all the surgery methods are suitable for everyone. Some require you to have very small breasts to begin with.

Many trans and non-binary people are keen to minimise the size and shape of their surgery scars and want them to be as hidden as possible. So there is information here about different ways to take care of scars. But this isn't true for everyone, and it's fine if you're not bothered by the look of your scars.

Chest reconstruction is known by a few different names, including top surgery and gender reassignment surgery (which could refer to top or lower surgery). Plus, each of the different surgery methods has more than one name, so it can be difficult to keep track. The following pages use common names for the surgeries, but other names they might be known by are mentioned also.

Chest reconstruction is different to a breast reduction. A breast reduction makes the breasts smaller but aims to keep enough size and shape so the breasts are seen as female.

The different methods for chest reconstruction
Liposuction

Liposuction involves making a small incision, about four milli-metres long, on either side of the chest to remove the required amount of fat tissue to flatten the chest. Breast tissue is not removed. Liposuction is only used for chest reconstruction when someone has very small breasts and good skin elasticity, meaning the skin will retain its shape without sagging after some of the inner tissue is taken out.

The advantage of liposuction is it can often leave no visible scars and leaves sensitivity to the nipples. The disadvantage is it is not suitable for most people due to the size of the breasts.

Sometimes liposuction will be used alongside one of the other surgery methods covered here to remove extra fat and create a more even appearance on both sides of the chest.

Keyhole method

The keyhole method is similar to liposuction. It is also only suit-able for people with very small breasts and good skin elasticity. In this surgery, the surgeon makes an incision around half the cir-cumference of the areola and uses this small opening to remove enough tissue to reshape the chest. Again, the advantage is the scarring is minimal and hidden and nipple sensitivity is retained, but the disadvantage is it's not suitable for most people.

Peri-areolar method

The peri-areolar method involves cutting a "doughnut" shape of skin from around the nipple and using this incision to give the surgeon access to the fat tissue underneath in order to remove it. The outer edge of the doughnut is then drawn in using a "purse-string" stitch.

The advantages of this surgery are you can keep the feeling in the nipples and the scar is fairly hidden, at the edge of the nipple. The disadvantage is, like liposuction, it is not suitable for most people because you need to have a small chest to begin with. Also, because of how the skin is "drawn in", it can leave puckering around the nipple. Mostly this puckering smooths out over the weeks after surgery. But there is a risk that you will be left with some puckering. This surgery has a high rate of people asking for revisions.

Peri-areolar is also called peri, circumareolar or the doughnut incision.

Peri-areolar method

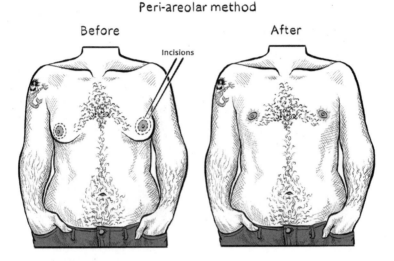

Before · After · Incisions

Double mastectomy

Mastectomy means "removing a breast", so a double mastectomy means removing both breasts. It is the most common form of chest reconstruction for trans and non-binary people.

The double mastectomy involves a curved incision in the fold under each breast, and a curved incision across the top of the breasts, mirroring it. The breast gland along with skin and fat is removed, and the two incisions are pulled together to create a scar along the edge of the pectoral muscle, where there is a natural fold. The nipples are attached to the section of skin that is removed, so these are removed, resized and sewn onto the chest in a new position, in a procedure known as nipple grafting. Nipples are usually resized to around 2–2.5 cm across.

The advantage of this surgery is it's suitable for all breast sizes and for people with less elastic skin. It can result in a flat, smooth chest appearance with well-proportioned nipples. The disadvantage is it leaves a long, large scar from under the armpit to around the centre of the sternum. This scar is likely to slowly fade with time and might also get hidden a bit with chest hair around it, especially if you are taking testosterone.

Double mastectomy method

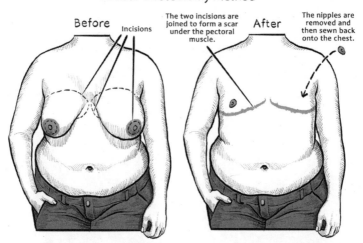

A double mastectomy for chest reconstruction is different to the double mastectomy performed on people who have breast cancer. A double mastectomy for trans and non-binary people has an aesthetic aim. Some of the fat and tissue is kept under the skin so the final appearance is seen as a male.

A double mastectomy can also be called bilateral mastectomy.

Inverted T and buttonhole methods

The "inverted T" and "buttonhole" methods are very similar to each other. For the inverted T method, an incision is made around the nipple, but the nipple is kept attached to the body by a string of tissue underneath (this connection is called a pellicle). A further incision is made in a line down from the nipple, and along the underside of the chest, in a similar way to the double mastectomy.

The advantage of this method is that you keep feeling in the nipple, and there is no risk of a nipple graft not taking. The disadvantages are there is an extra scar, and there isn't the option to reposition the nipple.

The buttonhole method is very similar to the inverted T, but instead of having the extra visible scar running vertically down from the nipple, the surgeon creates a horizontal incision in the skin where the nipple would be appropriately placed, and pops the nipple through from the underside, like putting a button through a buttonhole. This technique works well for people who need more tissue removed than is possible using keyhole surgery or liposuction, and also people who want to retain nipple sensation.

Inverted T method

Before   After

Incisions

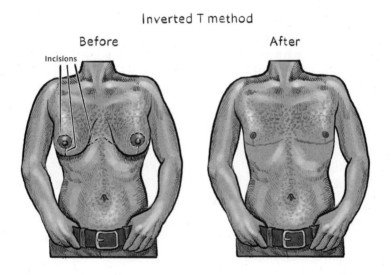

Not all surgeons perform every method of surgery. So if there is one method you prefer, you will need to ask to be referred to a surgeon who performs it. But bear in mind that not all surgeries are suitable for all people. Your surgeon will advise you on which surgical technique will give you the best result. Remember that only people with very small breasts to begin with are likely to be offered the liposuction method that can leave no scar.

If you disagree with one surgeon's perspective on the best technique for you, you can go for a consultation with more than one surgeon.

Nipple grafts

For a double mastectomy, the nipples will be removed entirely and grafted back onto the body. This will reduce their sensitivity, and afterwards they can feel just like the rest of the skin around them. If losing the feeling in your nipples is your main concern, ask your surgeon if you can have one of the procedures that does not remove the nipple entirely.

Nipple tattoos

Sometimes a nipple graft does not "take". This happens when, after the nipple is sewn back on, the blood flow is not fully restored and the graft either partly or fully comes away. This isn't painful but can leave you with a nipple that is an odd shape, or that is missing altogether. Under the nipple will just be plain skin.

If this happens, one option is to have nipple tattooing. This can give a permanent image of a nipple on the body, to fill in any gaps where the circular shape of the nipple is missing or replace a whole nipple.

Nipple tattoos can look three dimensional, but they won't feel three dimensional to the touch. They can give you more confidence if the appearance of your nipples makes you uncomfortable.

Always look at a tattoo artist's work and check their experience and qualifications before booking a session.

Double mastectomy and hysterectomy at the same time

Some surgeons offer the option of having chest reconstruction at the same time as a hysterectomy, a surgery that removes internal organs from the uterine reproductive system. This could include all or some of the uterus (womb), fallopian tubes, ovaries, cervix and vagina. See Chapter 5 on hysterectomies for more information on this surgery. Having both surgeries at the same time can be done so long as the surgeon has the experience required in chest contouring. Both double mastectomy and hysterectomy are major operations, and having both done at the same time can take a larger toll on your body, and mean a longer recovery time.

Your surgeon may ask you to stop smoking in the weeks leading up to the surgery and for some weeks afterward.

Alternatives to chest reconstruction

If you are under the age requirement for surgery, are on a long waiting list or saving up the cost, there are a few ways you can flatten your chest.

Chest binder

A chest binder is worn under your clothes (without a bra) and squashes the chest against your skin to give the appearance of a male chest. You can buy chest binders designed for trans and non-binary people at stores online from brands such as Underworks, gc2b and Paxsies. You can also make your own binder from strips of extra wide elastic (10 cm wide or more) sewn in a loop.

Sports bra

A sports bra can create a similar flattened effect as a binder but gives a bit more support to your chest. This can be a good option for people with larger chests who find wearing a binder uncomfortable or impractical. Also, a chest binder shouldn't be worn while exercising, whereas some sports bras are designed for vigorous exercise.

Another option is a swimming costume, the kind that doesn't support the breasts. They can be cheap to pick up, but bear in mind you have to take them off every time you need to pee unless you adapt them.

Take care when binding. How flat you can make your chest will depend on the size you are to begin with. It can be tempting to bind extra tight to get a flatter chest. But binding too tightly risks restricting your breathing, rib fractures and damage to your skin because not enough air is able to get to your skin. If you are binding, remember:

- Do not bind with bandages or tape, as these have been shown to have the most risk of causing damage.
- Take breaks from binding every six to eight hours at least.
- Do not wear your binder when sleeping.
- Wash and dry your binder regularly.
- Take a binding break if your skin becomes sore or itchy.
- Look after the skin under the binder. If you develop a rash or soreness, let it heal before binding again.
- Take extra care when binding in hot weather.

Binding healthily involves a balance – some compression to change the appearance of your torso and reduce gender dysphoria, but not so much as to damage your body.

Going for a consultation

Once you have been referred to a surgical service, you will be invited for a consultation with the surgeon. This is sometimes several weeks or months before the surgery itself. A consultation is a chance for your surgeon to explain the procedures they perform and what to expect, and for you to ask any questions. It can sometimes be difficult to know where to start when it comes to asking your surgeon questions, so we have listed some below. There is also space at the end of the book to jot down your own questions.

- What different methods are right for me?
- Do I have the option to keep sensitivity in my nipples?
- I have a long-term health condition; how will it impact the surgery and my recovery?
- I take medication; how will that impact the surgery and my recovery?
- When can the surgery be scheduled? What if I need it rescheduled?
- How much does the surgery cost, and what does that cover? Do you take my health insurance?

- If there are complications and I need a second surgery, does the original payment cover that?
- How do you take payment, and is it possible to pay in instalments?
- How long will I be in hospital?
- How long should I take off work or study?
- How long have you been performing chest reconstruction? How many procedures have you done?
- What qualifications do you have? What training do you have? Are you a member of a relevant professional association?
- Can I see photos of your recent work?
- Have you worked with trans and non-binary people previously?
- What complications can occur, and how likely are they?
- What will it look like straight out of surgery, and how will it change over time?
- What should I do if I am not happy with the result?
- What aftercare do you provide?
- Do I need to do anything in preparation for surgery?

During the consultation the surgeon may want to examine you, in order to assess if you are suitable for the surgery you are interested in. This could mean being seen topless. If you will find this too difficult, contact the surgical service ahead of time and ask if there are other options.

Getting ready for surgery

After the surgery, you will probably find it difficult to raise your arms, so you might want a couple of changes of clothes that you don't need to pull over your head. Aim to wear loose, soft clothing that won't press or irritate your chest. In hospital you might want a dressing gown, cardigan or zip-up hoodie for warmth. Plus, the doctors and nurses will want to check your wound sites each day, so it's useful to wear clothes that fasten at the front.

You won't be able to drive yourself home after the surgery. It's a good idea to have someone with you when you travel home, for support and to carry your bags, as you shouldn't carry heavy objects.

Being in hospital

Top surgery lasts between one and a half and four hours, depending which technique you have. When you come round, you will have dressings across your chest and will probably find it difficult to sit up. In order to help your body heal and to not pull on the stitches, try not to move too much.

You may have drains attached when you wake up. Drains are thin plastic tubes that are placed under your skin along the length of the incision. The tubes are attached to plastic containers that will steadily fill with a small quantity of blood that is draining from the wound site.

You may be asked to wear a compression binder for a few weeks after the surgery to help the swelling go down.

You will be visited regularly by nurses after your surgery, to check your dressings, blood pressure and pain levels. You will also probably be seen by the doctor. You may want to ask some questions such as:

- How did it go?
- Were there any complications?
- When can the drains come out?
- Can I walk around the hospital?
- When can I shower?
- When can I go home?
- Do I have to come back to the hospital for a check-up, and when?

Recovery

It can take around one to two weeks to recover from chest reconstruction before going back to an office job, and four to six weeks to recover before going back to an active job or doing sport. During this time, avoid lifting and carrying heavy objects or exercising vigorously, especially exercise that involves your arms, such as swimming or weightlifting. This is to help your wounds heal and reduce the size of the scars.

What to do if you're unhappy with the result

Some people find they are not happy with the result of their top surgery. Your chest may look bigger and uneven at first, but bear in mind after the surgery it will take a while for the swelling to go down and the area to even out. However, if you are unhappy with the results, you can ask your GP to be referred back to the surgeon to discuss a revision. If you had surgery privately, contact the hospital and ask for a consultation to follow up on your surgery.

Breast cancer

If you have had chest reconstruction, the risk of breast cancer is reduced, but it isn't entirely gone. Cisgender men, trans and non-binary people all have some breast tissue. Without any surgery, the rates of breast cancer in people born with breasts is 1 in 8.[1] For comparison, the rates in people born with a penis is around 1 in 800.[2]

Chest reconstruction for trans and non-binary people is not the same as a mastectomy to remove the breast because of cancer. During chest reconstruction, a significant amount of chest tissue is left behind, but it is sculpted into a different shape. After chest reconstruction, continue to check your chest for lumps and book an appointment with your doctor if you find anything unusual.

Taking testosterone has not been found to lead to a higher risk of developing breast cancer.

---

1   NHS (2023). Breast Cancer in Women. www.nhs.uk/conditions/breast-cancer
2   American Cancer Society (2023). Key Statistics for Breast Cancer in Men. www.cancer.org/cancer/breast-cancer-in-men/about/key-statistics.html

How to check for lumps

There is no right or wrong way to check for lumps. The aim is to get to know your chest, how it looks and feels, and check regularly for any changes.

Look at your chest and feel each side, from in your armpit up to your collarbone. It can be easier to do this in the shower or bath, when your skin is slippery. You can also look at your chest in the mirror. Look with your arms by your side and also with them raised.

Final thing

Chest surgery is expensive if you have to pay for it yourself, and it can be difficult to cope while you're waiting and saving up. Lots of people will be struggling with this at the same time you are, so it can be helpful to find friends in person or online who are going through the same thing and support each other.

FINN'S STORY

I spoke to Finn, 39, about having chest reconstruction using the liposuction method ten years ago.

I was never very big in the first place and I never felt a huge amount of distress about it all, but I wanted to walk around topless and feel comfortable.

I remember going in for a consultation, and that was a bit awkward. My pitch was I wanted to have peri, because that's what I thought the option was for people with smaller chests. His pitch was bilateral mastectomy. I said I want to retain my nipples, cause they're really sensitive.

We had a bit of a discussion and he said he could do the same keyhole surgery he does for cisgender men who have gynaecomastia.[3] That sounded good to me because if this is what cisgender men have, of course I want that.

---

3   Gynaecomastia is a common condition that causes boys' and men's breasts to swell and become larger than normal.
Citation: https://www.nhs.uk/common-health-questions/mens-health/what-is-gynaecomastia

After the surgery I wasn't 100 per cent happy, because it felt like not much had changed. The surgeon said he'd taken about a teacup of fat out of each side. I thought, that's not very much! But he said taking too much would look unnatural, and if I wanted to have a completely flat chest, I'd just need to lose weight. Bear in mind at the time I was at least ten kilos overweight, so he had a fair point.

The worst part was I had to wear a binder for another six weeks. Part of the joy of top surgery is you burn that damn thing and you never want to wear anything like it again. So then to be made to wear a surgical binder for another six weeks – I was like, seriously?

My recuperation was relatively quick though. The first time I left the house after surgery, I felt quite weak. I remember taking a lot of codeine and listening to a lot of music and just being a bit out of it. Then after about a week I had a shower, which I think everyone was grateful for.

Something I've learnt in the years following surgery is to sculpt the look I want I needed to lose some weight by exercising and eating better, and I needed to build up my pectoral muscles. It couldn't just all be down to surgery; surgery only does part of it.

I remember going on holiday in June, four months after surgery. Being topless in public for the first time by the pool was really scary because I just felt everyone would look at me and see what I thought I saw, because I thought I still saw breasts in the mirror. It was hard to realise that people were probably not even noticing, and to get over that psychological hurdle and just go for a swim.

It definitely took time to see what I actually look like in the mirror. Even now I often look in the mirror thinking, is that me? I haven't quite caught up in some respects. I'm still a little bit surprised when clothes fit me properly on the top half of my torso. I think I get haunted by how my body used to look. I look in the mirror and I'm expecting to see this pre-transition young person and I'm thinking, who's that old man?

And there's an interesting thing about scarring. On the

one hand I'm really grateful I didn't have any scars, but on the other hand it plays into this "I'm not trans enough" thing I sometimes feel, because I don't have the big trans surgery scars. It kind of makes me feel like I'm not part of that club. When I'm on Grindr I have some guys basically saying, no you're not trans, you don't have any scars. I'm like, I am, trust me. There's so much of a culture around that very particular big scar.

One thing I was really worried about was that my areolas were too big. I think, particularly in trans culture, we have these ideas of what men look like, that men are flat-chested and that everyone's nipples are the same sort of size. I did a bit of research on Google just to see as many different chests as possible and realised there are some men that have big areolas. It was really good to see there's huge diversity in what chests look like. I think too often we can look at each other's surgery results and think that's what ours should look like too, even though that might not be optimal for us.

5

Hysterectomy

A hysterectomy is an operation to remove the uterus and some of the surrounding organs and tissues. There is more than one type of hysterectomy, and different parts are removed depending on which type you have.

Some trans and non-binary people have a hysterectomy without having any other lower surgery, but it can also be done as a stage of lower surgery, for either metoidioplasty or phalloplasty.

Types of hysterectomy

The type of hysterectomy you have depends on your reason for having it. The main types of hysterectomy (sometimes called "hysto") are:

- **Total hysterectomy**. The uterus and cervix are removed.
- **Subtotal hysterectomy**. The main part of the uterus is removed, leaving the cervix.
- **Total hysterectomy with bilateral salpingo-oophorectomy**. This means the uterus, cervix, fallopian tubes and ovaries are removed. Removing the fallopian tubes is called a salpingectomy, and removing the ovaries is an oophorectomy.
- **Radical hysterectomy**. The uterus and surrounding tissues are removed, including the fallopian tubes, part of the vagina, the ovaries, the lymph glands and fatty tissue.

Ovarian reproductive system

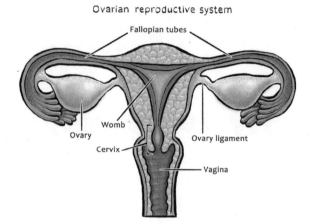

It is also possible to have the whole of the vagina removed during a hysterectomy. You might choose this if you think it would decrease your gender dysphoria. If this is something you're interested in, it would be something to discuss with your surgeon at your consultation.

The vagina can be removed by a vaginectomy. Or the surgeon may use a method called colpocleisis. During a colpocleisis, the vagina is not removed but the walls are stitched together so it is no longer a tube.

Why you would have a hysterectomy

A hysterectomy is sometimes used to solve chronic gynaecological problems, so some trans and non-binary people will have already had one before considering any gender-affirming surgery. Or you may be offered one to address a medical problem unrelated to your gender identity. For example, a hysterectomy may be used to solve:

- heavy periods
- fibroids
- prolapse of the uterus – when part of the uterus bulges down into the vagina
- cancer of the uterus, ovaries or cervix.

Different forms of hysterectomy are options for trans and non-binary people, depending on what their main aim is.

- A hysterectomy that removes the cervix takes away the need to have cervical smears, which can be triggering for gender dysphoria.
- A hysterectomy that removes the ovaries causes periods to stop. You might choose this if you are not taking testosterone, or you do but still have breakthrough bleeding.
- A hysterectomy can reduce gender dysphoria that is triggered just from having any of the uterine reproductive organs.
- A hysterectomy can be a stage in the process towards having metoidioplasty or phalloplasty surgery. Depending on whether you are having metoidioplasty or phalloplasty, you may need to have a hysterectomy in a different way, so see the chapters (Chapters 8 and 9) on those surgeries for more information.

However, you do not need to have a hysterectomy to prevent cancer or other illnesses. Taking testosterone as hormone therapy has not been found to damage the ovarian reproductive organs.

Thinking ahead

If you plan to have a vaginectomy as part of meta (metoidioplasty) or phallo (phalloplasty) surgery, you will need the type that removes the uterus and cervix. This is because without a vagina you can no longer have a smear test, because it is performed through the vagina.

You're advised to get the hysterectomy done in advance of meta or phallo surgery. Some surgeons offer to perform the hysterectomy at the same time as the metoidioplasty, but this can make the vaginectomy more complicated. It is recommended that you have the hysterectomy at least three months prior to having metoidioplasty.

If you are considering a hysterectomy, but are unsure yet

whether you will later have further lower surgery, let your surgeon know you may want further surgery in the future. Tissues that you might need for future genital reconstruction can be left in place. For example, a portion of the vagina can be left during vaginectomy so it can be used if you choose to have urethra lengthening later, as part of phalloplasty or metoidioplasty.

Having a hysterectomy can permanently remove your options for having a baby, either from being pregnant yourself or using a surrogate. A surrogate is when someone else is pregnant with a baby that uses eggs from your ovaries. It is possible to freeze eggs and use them later. See Chapter 13: Fertility, Contraception and Having a Baby for more information.

How the surgery is performed

There are three different methods for performing a hysterectomy. They are all performed under general anaesthetic:

- **Laparoscopic hysterectomy.** Also known as keyhole surgery. This is when the uterus and other organs are removed through several small cuts in the belly. This method can leave small scars, each around 1 cm long.
- **Vaginal hysterectomy.** In this method, the uterus and any other organs are removed through a cut in the top of the vagina. The organs are then removed through the vagina.
- **Abdominal hysterectomy.** In this method, a wide cut is made through the lower belly.

Vaginal and laparoscopic surgery may be better for trans or non-binary people considering having further lower surgery. Both methods don't disrupt the abdominal wall, which may be used in other lower surgeries.

Recovery

A hysterectomy is a major operation. Even if you have the operation laparoscopically or vaginally and cannot see large incisions, you still need time to recover. Expect to be in hospital at least overnight, and sometimes for a few days. It then takes around six to eight weeks to recover.

While in recovery, rest as much as possible, and avoid lifting heavy items like shopping. However, you are also encouraged to start taking short walks from the day after surgery to reduce the risk of deep vein thrombosis (DVT), caused from being still for long periods of time.

Prepare your home ahead of time for when you come out of hospital, such as:

- Stock up on easy to make, healthy food.
- Stock up on heavy items you need, such as pet food, cans, soda and milk.
- Stock up on essentials such as loo roll so you don't need to go to the shops so often.
- Have some plasters, antibacterial wash, gauze, surgical tape and paracetamol in the bathroom in case you have any bleeding and pain. The hospital will probably send you home with painkillers or a prescription.
- Let a friend know you are having surgery so you have someone to contact if you need help.

There are no known surgical risks specific to trans and non-binary people having a hysterectomy. The risks are the same for anyone having the surgery. They include:

- bleeding
- infection
- damage to the ureter – the ureter is the tube that carries urine from the kidneys to the bladder. Damage to the ureter is a rare complication. If it is damaged, it is usually repaired during the hysterectomy. This happens in 1 in every 1000 cases[1]
- damage to the bladder or bowel – this rarely happens.

1   NHS (2023). Hysterectomy. www.nhs.uk/conditions/hysterectomy/risks

It can lead to infection or incontinence, but it can also sometimes be repaired during the hysterectomy if damage is done

- ovary problems – if one or both of your ovaries is left intact, it or they could still stop working properly within five years, because ovaries receive some of their blood supply from the uterus
- vaginal problems – if you have a vaginal hysterectomy, there is a risk of problems to the top of the vaginal canal, nearest to the uterus. It could lead to prolapse in later years.

If you have kept your vagina after having a hysterectomy, you may have some bleeding or discharge from the vagina for the first four to six weeks after the surgery. It should be less than a regular period. This is normal, but contact your GP if you have heavy bleeding or discharge with a bad smell.

If you use your vagina during sex, it is best to wait until after your scars have healed and any discharge and bleeding has stopped before using it again.

If your uterus has been removed, you will no longer be able to get pregnant, but if you use your vagina for sex, you can still catch a sexually transmitted disease, whatever the gender of your partner. See Chapter 16: Sexual Health and Check-Ups for more information.

Effect of hysterectomy on hormone balance

One effect of having your ovaries removed is you will no longer be producing as much oestrogen. Most of the oestrogen produced by people with a uterine reproductive system is from the ovaries. But oestrogen is also produced in fatty tissue, in certain bone cells and in the brain. (People with penile reproductive systems also produce oestrogen from these places.)

The reduction of oestrogen can have an impact on your bone density, so it is important to follow up with your endocrinologist after having ovaries removed to check your testosterone levels and see if they need adjusting.

Final thing

Some people experience fluctuations in mood after hysterectomy, which might be due to the changes in hormone levels after the ovaries are removed. Whatever the reason, be kind to yourself after having a hysterectomy.

JON'S STORY

Jon transitioned as a young person and had a hysterectomy when he was 17. Jon talked to me about his decision to have a hysterectomy and the traumatic complications that happened after the surgery.

I started on testosterone when I was 16 and a year later I had a full hysterectomy, mainly due to breakthrough bleeding. I've had two surgeries: top surgery and a hysterectomy. For me, the hysterectomy was a more important SRS[2] surgery. I just felt really uncomfortable having all those organs inside me. I didn't want to ever get a smear test in the future. I have weird undiagnosed vaginal pain, it could be atrophy or something else, and it doesn't really bother me day to day, but it is there. So I thought let's just get the whole thing out.

I prepared by getting some baggy clothes and a portable phone charger, things like that. I thought, let's make sure I don't have to walk far because I'll be in my bedroom for a while. With top surgery you can walk around fairly normally afterwards, but with hysto you can't always. Even though you're encouraged to move, you can't really move far.

The fear for me was I'd be catheterised. Because of the vaginal pain I've had, that area is super sensitive. I don't want to touch it, I don't want anyone else touching it, so I was scared. I was thinking, are they going to stick a tube up my pee hole? What pain am I going to be in then? But actually I couldn't feel it at all. It felt a bit strange, but I wasn't in pain from it.

So surgery went great, until I realised I was bleeding

---

2   Sex reassignment surgery.

everywhere. The surgeon had to be called and I was wheeled immediately back into surgery because I was bleeding out. I remember being in a panic not knowing what was happening, looking up at everyone just thinking, help. There was a guy standing over me, the anaesthesiologist, and he said, "Don't worry, are you ready?" and I said, "I guess." And then I was out for the second time.

So I had two surgeries, two general anaesthetics, in the space of a very short amount of time, which wasn't great. I definitely felt horrible after I woke up, not anything like top surgery. I was really sick. There's a photo on my Facebook and my face looks grey.

Directly after the surgery it felt like I'd been kicked in the stomach by a rhinoceros. I don't know if it was worse from having two surgeries on the same site, but I was fucked.

I've always been a big fan of procrastination, so doing nothing during the recovery was great for me. I got into gaming, I played Lord of the Rings online obsessively during that period of time; that was fantastic.

I was back at work after twelve weeks. I didn't really feel normal but I started going back to work. It took a while. Hysterectomy fucked me up. Even now my body is different. I can still feel twinges if I overexert myself. I don't want to strain or do any real heavy lifting; I want to protect that area. It's a big old surgery I had. And even though my insides are probably stitched up tighter than any stitching they'd ever done because I had to have that extra surgery, it's always in the back of my mind that I've had this major surgery.

And I'm a worrier. I'm scared of prolapse and something going wrong internally because I don't have that support from the cervix anymore. I'm working on my pelvic floor muscles. They protect your pelvic floor and strengthen your core, which is key for keeping your insides where they're meant to be.

It's probably the last surgery I will have. I'm not interested in lower surgery, especially after what I went through with the hysto. It's not something I want to repeat on my lower extremities. Kudos to those who do, but it's not for me.

It's so weird to look back on my transition. I was calculating it and in two years I will have lived longer as a man than I ever did as a girl essentially, because I transitioned at 16. How many trans people back in the day were able to say that? I think it's good for people to hear from a trans person who transitioned at 16 and who's now 30. Because as a young person I made the right decision. Young trans people don't disappear off the face of the earth; we grow into fine and well-adjusted trans adults.

6

Facial Feminisation Surgery

This chapter is a bit different to previous chapters, because "facial feminisation surgery" (FFS) is not just one surgery but a range of different ones. Which you choose to have, if any, is down to your own perceptions and dissatisfaction with your face and throat.

You do not need to have a certain kind of face to be a woman or to "look like" a woman. Your face is not wrong. When the phrase "facial feminisation" is used here that's partly just because that's what the surgery is generally called. But it's also because this surgery is about *perception*, and in this case, the perception of femininity.

You could say the same thing about breast augmentation. It is not about what is or isn't feminine; it is about what is perceived, by other people and ourselves, as feminine. And "feminine" means whatever is considered feminine in the time you are living, in the country and culture you are in.

Surgery to your face is a big step. If you are thinking about surgery, consider first the difference changes in your voice and body language may have on how you are perceived. Plus, the changes to your face from oestrogen can take a few years to fully take effect. Surgery is expensive and often irreversible, whereas changes to your voice and body language are more under your control.

If you're taking oestrogen, it will affect the soft tissues of the body – the softness of your skin, fat distribution, hair growth and muscle. But it doesn't affect bone structure. And while taking oestrogen can slow or stop hair loss from your head, it won't cause new hair to grow. Changes to your face from oestrogen can begin around three months after starting it, but can take up to two years for the full effects to be seen.

Facial feminisation surgeries include:

- lipofilling
- hair line lowering
- forehead or brow contouring
- cheek augmentation
- Adam's apple reduction
- rhinoplasty (nose reshaping)
- lower jaw angle reduction.

Other surgeries you can find listed as facial feminisation are lip reshaping, chin reshaping, hair transplants and surgery to fix an over-bite or under-bite.

Some of these are known by different names in different countries, or between different clinics. New surgical options and methods are being developed all the time, so you may find new options also available when you start to explore.

Each of the surgeries that can fall into "facial feminisation" change the shape and size of one of the facial features. But what is possible to achieve will vary between people, depending on the underlying anatomy you have, the thickness of your skin and any previous injuries.

Faces and gender

Our faces are made up of different parts, and some parts more than others have a role in the gender we are seen as. While facial surgeons understand the subtle differences in faces that change them from being read as female or male, it is not an exact science. FFS aims to change the gender you are seen as by working on the areas of the face that have the biggest differences between being seen as male and seen as female: the forehead, around the eyes, the nose, the jaw, the chin and the Adam's apple.[1]

Faces and attractiveness

Keep in mind the difference between a face being read as male or female and "attractiveness". What is considered attractive or beautiful in a face varies across time, in different cultures and in different ethnicities. It is fair to say that there is a beauty standard, and we're probably all aware of it. But this beauty standard is not a truth, and different people find different features beautiful. Many of us – cisgender and transgender – struggle with accepting how we measure up against the beauty standard, and whether we look the way we want to look.

Having FFS is not surgery to make you more beautiful. The goal is for you to be recognised as female.

Preparing for surgery

Before any facial surgery, you will need to stop having any electrolysis, or hair plucking and waxing, from anywhere on your body, in order to reduce the risk of infection.

You may be asked to stop smoking two to four weeks before your surgery and for up to twelve weeks afterwards. It is unlikely you will need to stop taking hormones.

For any of the surgeries, it is helpful to build up a collection of photographs of the kinds of changes you are looking for to take to your surgeon. The more information you can give your surgeon, the better. Collect images of front and profile views.

---

1   Fisher, M., Lu, S.M., Chen, K., Zhang, B., Di Maggio M. and Bradley, J.P. (2020). Facial feminization surgery changes perception of patient gender. *Aesthetic Surgery Journal, 40*(7), 703–709. doi: 10.1093/asj/sjz303. PMID: 31676906

Language in this chapter

This chapter talks in a general way about the way "men" and "women" look. This is not to say that women can't have a feature, such as a large jaw, that is more typical on men. But the aim of this chapter is to talk about the features that are typically *seen* as male or female, and how FFS can change how your face is seen.

Many of these surgeries are often done together, and what combination you choose to have is up to you and the changes you want. The combination you have will affect the risk of complications, hospital inpatient time, recovery and time off work. That's why the information here is kept quite general.

Lipofilling
Why it's done

Lipofilling involves adding tiny amounts of fat to the face where there are hollows or sunken areas. It can be used in several areas of the face to give it a more feminine appearance either on its own or alongside another procedure to help smooth over an area where there was surgery on the bone and cartilage. This is also called fat grafting.

How it's done

Lipofilling involves taking a small amount of fat from one area of the body where there is plenty, such as the thighs or tummy, and injecting it into another part. The fat is removed with a very thin tube – a cannula or micro-cannula – purified and then injected into another area. Usually 1 cc of fat may be removed at a time, and then injected in tiny portions, 1/20 of a cc at a time, into an area of the face. There are no incisions or stitches needed.

Lipofilling can be used as part of FFS for cheek augmentation, for reducing the protrusion of the eye sockets, for filling in the temporal fossa (the depressions in the skull at the temples), making the forehead more oval in shape and for filling around the chin and in the lips. Lipofilling with fat from your own body lasts longer than using a dermal filler such as hyaluronic acid, which only lasts several months.

Fat cells are living tissue and need a blood supply to survive. When fat is transferred to another part of the body, around 50–70 per cent of the fat cells survive, so the surgeon may transfer more than is required initially, to compensate for this loss.

What it's like

Lipofilling is a day surgery if performed on its own. If it's part of a combination of different procedures on the face, you may be in hospital longer. And if a large area is being treated, you may need two sessions.

Lipofilling takes around an hour, if it isn't being done as part of another surgery, and is usually performed under general anaesthetic. Usually you can go home straight afterwards. So long as you are feeling well, you won't need to take time off work.

Risk

Lipofilling is considered a low-risk surgery, but there is a risk that you won't be happy with the results.

Hairline lowering

Why it's done

There are three features of the forehead that tend to differ between men and women. The distance between the hairline and the eyebrows tends to be smaller for women, meaning women have a smaller forehead with both their hairline lower and their eyebrows higher. Women's eyebrows typically lie above the upper rim of their eye sockets. Plus, men can lose their hair around their temples, even from a young age, giving their foreheads and hairline a distinctive shape.

Hairline lowering surgery aims to bring the hairline down to give you a smaller forehead. Some surgery options can include reshaping the hair loss around the temples at the same time. This is also sometimes known as forehead lowering, forehead reduction, hairline advancement, hairline correction and foreheadplasty.

How it's done

During the surgery, an incision is made at the meeting point of the hair-bearing and non-hair-bearing skin. The skin is then raised, brought forward and secured into its new position, and excess forehead skin is removed. Sometimes hair implants may also be used if there has been lots of hair lost at the temples.

This surgery only changes the way the skin and hairline lie; it does not affect the shape of the bone of your forehead. See "forehead contouring" below for surgery that changes the bone shape.

If you are having your hairline lowered to reduce the appearance of thinning hair around the temples, sometimes more than one surgery is necessary. The skin can only be brought forward so much in one surgery. Surgeons recommend waiting at least a year between advancements to allow the skin to loosen up enough to be stretched forward a second time.

What it's like

Hairline lowering is performed under general anaesthetic, and you will probably spend at least one night in hospital if you are having this procedure on its own, and possibly more if combined with other procedures. You will have stitches and staples in your scalp after the surgery, which will be removed after four to six days.

Surgeons recommend not washing your hair until after your first post-op appointment, and not use hair dye or any hair treatments until all the scabs have come off the incision line. There can be numbness around the area, so it is advised to not use a hair dryer, as you may not feel how hot it is and can risk burning your scalp.

Risks

As the incisions are placed in the hairline, the aim is to make them as invisible as possible, but all incisions leave a scar. Scars usually fade with time. Healing takes around seven to ten days, but it can take six weeks or more for the final result to be achieved. There are products on the market that are designed to minimise scarring. However, the side effects can sometimes be hair loss, so they are not suitable for this surgery.

Forehead contouring
Why it's done

Men often have a large, prominent forehead, referred to as "frontal bossing", and a flatter upper forehead, whereas women often have a smoother, curved forehead.

Brow contouring surgery aims to reduce the "bossing" to give a smoother curve and less prominent ridge above the eye sockets, and raise the eyebrows slightly above the rim of the eye socket.

How it's done

People have different forehead structures. Some people have a frontal sinus cavity, an air-filled space above the nose and eyes, but others don't. So there are different techniques for performing this surgery, depending on your anatomy. The incision for forehead contouring is usually across the top of the head, just behind the hairline, from ear to ear. This way it can be hidden in your hairline.

Foreheads are sometimes reshaped just by burring or shaving the bone away. Another technique is to remove the frontal sinus bone of the forehead and reshape it, then fit it back into the skull. Sometimes extra materials will be used, such as very thin titanium plates, held in place with miniature screws.

A surgeon should use non-magnetic materials to hold the bone in place, meaning they won't interfere with an MRI or airport security.

What it's like

This surgery is performed under general anaesthetic, and usually involves an overnight stay in hospital. The swelling and bruising usually goes down in ten to twelve days.

Risks

If you have material added to your forehead, such as a metal plate, this can sometimes get infected. You may need to have the piece removed and replaced. Because the supraorbital nerve is usually cut during this surgery, it is common to experience numbness in the forehead. Sometimes it is permanent, but the majority of the time, the feeling returns.

If you wear a helmet for work, or regularly wear a motorcycle helmet, these put pressure on your forehead. It is recommended to take longer off work to give your forehead more time to heal before wearing anything that puts pressure on the area. Surgeons recommend six to seven weeks to avoid creating a deformity.

Cheek augmentation
Why it's done
The aim of cheek augmentation is to give the cheeks a fuller, more rounded look. Cheek augmentation can be achieved with either lipofilling or cheek implants.

For lipofilling, the process is the same as described in the section on lipofilling. The small injections of fat are added around the cheeks. This procedure rarely has side effects.

If you are having several surgeries to your face as part of facial feminisation, some surgeons recommend having cheek augmentation done last. This is because facial feminisation often involves making parts of the face smaller, so after these surgeries are done, the cheeks will be proportionally larger. That change in proportion may be enough. The goal with facial surgery should always be to maintain a balance across the whole face. This surgery is sometimes also known as cheek enhancement.

How it's done
Cheek implant surgery is performed by making incisions inside the mouth, to avoid external scarring. An implant, usually made from silicone, is placed over the cheek bone. Another method is to make a cut in the lower eyelid to insert the cheek implant there. Dissolvable stitches will be used in your mouth.

Cheek implants come in a range of shapes, sizes and materials to suit different people. Silicone implants are fixed to the cheek with tiny, 8 mm screws. Custom-made cheek implants are occasionally available, but they cost much more than the "off the shelf" variety. Sometimes a surgeon will choose to do a combination of implants and lipofilling.

What it's like

Cheek implant surgery can be performed as an outpatient procedure, if you have it done as a single procedure, meaning you won't have to stay overnight. Sometimes the surgery is performed under local anaesthetic, but it is likely you will be given a general anaesthetic.

After the surgery, you should eat soft food that doesn't need a lot of chewing and chomping, and brush your teeth three times a day to remove bacteria from your mouth.

Risks

Numbness can be expected around the cheeks for a short while, but the feeling usually returns in a few weeks. It can also be difficult to speak, smile or yawn for a few days, due to the swelling.

The implants are rarely going to be perfectly fitted to your face and the edges may be visible, especially in the thin skin around the eyes.

Cheek implants can become infected and need to be removed. When this happens, without the implant, the cheek can sag, so you may need another implant or a cheek lift to fix it.

Adam's apple reduction
Why it's done

The aim of Adam's apple reduction surgery is to smooth down the Adam's apple so it does not stick out so much. People of all genders can have an Adam's apple that sticks out, but it is more common in men because they tend to have a larger larynx (voice box).

This is not voice changing surgery; the Adam's apple reduction only changes the appearance of the throat. There is another chapter on voice changing surgeries (Chapter 11: Vocal Surgery).

The larynx contains several areas of tough connective tissue and cartilage. The thyroid cartilage is the largest, and this is what we see as the Adam's apple. The surgery is often called a reduction laryngoplasty, or sometimes a trachea shave, but this is a bit misleading as it is neither the trachea that is reduced nor is it reduced by a shaving method.

How it's done

The surgery is performed under a general anaesthetic. The surgeon enters the throat either with an incision under the chin, in the submental crease, or directly through the neck in front of the Adam's apple. While using the submental chin crease requires more skill, going in through the neck can leave a visible scar that moves up and down as you swallow. Small pieces of the thyroid cartilage are then removed. The surgery can be performed on its own, or in combination with other facial surgeries. There is usually little swelling or bruising, which should go down in a few days.

Not everyone's anatomy is the same, and so it is not always possible for everyone to have a perfectly smooth throat after an Adam's apple reduction. At your consultation, your surgeon should be able to give you more information about what to expect from your anatomy. Sometimes it is possible to have a second reduction, but usually a surgeon will take as much as they can the first time.

What it's like

The surgery, when performed on its own, doesn't take very long, usually around an hour. You will probably stay one night in hospital and be able to go home with just a small bandage over the incision. As with all the surgeries, no heavy lifting or straining should be done during recovery, as this can cause bleeding.

Risks

As we get older, our cartilage ossifies, meaning it can harden into bone. So a risk for people over 30 years old is damage to the hardened cartilage in the throat, which can lead to a fracture.

Some people experience a temporary lowering of their voice, which is probably due to the swelling in the throat.

There is a risk of damage to your voice if too much of the cartilage is removed. Permanent voice loss is a rare but possible risk with this surgery, so ask your surgeon about their experience and their success rate to reduce your risk.

Rhinoplasty
Why it's done

Rhinoplasty is surgery to change the shape of the nose. Sometimes people call it a "nose job". As part of facial feminisation, it can adjust the shape of the nose to something seen as female. There are some general differences between male and female noses. Male noses tend to be larger and the top tends to be a straight line down to the tip, whereas female noses tend to have a slight scoop. Male noses tend to have a tip that points down or straight, whereas female noses tend to point up. The nostrils tend to be wider on men. Plus the tips of male noses tend to be larger and more bulbous.

None of these features are "male" or "female"; all people can have them. But if you are wanting your face to be seen as female, these changes can have a profound effect.

A dorsal hump – the bump that some people have in the middle of their nose – can be removed with rhinoplasty also. It is neither unattractive nor a mark of maleness or femaleness, but it can be removed if it bothers you.

Women of different ethnicities tend to have differently shaped noses. When speaking with your surgeon about feminising your face, ensure they are comfortable talking about different ethnicities and are not using a "one size fits all" Caucasian standard for what a woman's nose should look like.

How it's done

Rhinoplasty surgeries are performed either from inside the nostril (a closed rhinoplasty) or by making a small incision in the underside of the nose to lift up the skin (an open rhinoplasty). How it's performed depends on what type of changes the surgeon will make. There are pros and cons to both methods. An open rhinoplasty can leave a small scar in your columella, the piece of bone and cartilage that separates your nostrils. But a closed rhinoplasty can make it harder for the surgeon to see the areas they're working with.

Some surgeons insist on performing rhinoplasty and forehead contouring together, if you're planning on having forehead contouring as well. This way, changes to the shape of both parts can be done while maintaining the smooth relationship of the forehead to the nose. It is not necessary to have forehead surgery, if you don't want it, in order to have rhinoplasty. But if you are thinking about it, consider finding a surgeon who can do both.

What is possible with rhinoplasty depends on the bone and cartilage of the nose, the elasticity of the skin and your age. People with thinner skin are more likely to be able to have their nose remodelled, because the skin can drape easily over the new structure underneath. Thicker skin can find it harder to adapt to a new shape underneath.

The nose needs to have stopped growing before a surgeon will operate, which happens around 18 or 19 years of age. It can take around thirty days for recovery from rhinoplasty, but the complete results may not fully settle until eight to twelve months later.

What it's like

Feminising rhinoplasty is performed under general anaesthetic. You are likely to spend a night or two in hospital, and have a cast and a splint held over your nose for around seven days, along with other dressings and tape to protect your nose as it heals. This must be kept dry. You won't be able to blow your nose, so gauze is often tucked under the nose to catch any drips. You will breathe through your mouth for the first week, which can be uncomfortable.

There is likely to be bruising around the eyes, which will take around a couple of weeks to heal. As mentioned, an open rhinoplasty involves opening up the nose, so healing time will be longer. Sore noses and headaches can occur.

If you wear glasses, they cannot be worn at all for a month after rhinoplasty. Contact lenses are fine, but if you cannot wear them, you will need to hold your glasses up to see by.

Risks

As with all surgery, there is a risk of infection and bleeding. A rhinoplasty can also sometimes lead to permanent trouble breathing, damage to the cartilage wall between your nostrils or a change to your sense of smell. Ask your surgeon for more information about these risks.[2]

Lower jaw angle reduction
Why it's done

Typically, women have more tapered, curved jaws than men. The angle and size of the lower jaw, especially the angle below the ears, is usually larger and more rectangular in men. Lower jaw reduction aims to reduce the size of the jaw and smooth out the curve of the lower jaw.

How it's done

The lower jaw (the mandible) contains the teeth at the front and then goes all the way back and up to your ears. The corner of bone you can feel below your ears that moves as you chew is the mandibular angle. The masseter muscle, the muscle we use to chew, is attached at the back of the mandibular angle.

Lower jaw angle reduction works on three areas of the lower jaw: where the side of the jaw is wider and flares out, the pronounced mandibular angle at the back and the size of the muscle. Surgeons reach the bone and muscle by making incisions inside your mouth so there is no external scarring.

To reduce the flaring and size of the side of the jaw, the hard bone is burred down. How much can be removed is limited by the position of the roots of the teeth, which shouldn't be disturbed. The mandibular angle is smoothed into a smaller curve by cutting away the bone with a saw. And finally, some of the bulk inside the masseter muscle is removed. How much bone and muscle

---

2   NHS (2023). Rhinoplasty. www.nhs.uk/conditions/cosmetic-procedures/cosmetic-surgery/nose-reshaping-rhinoplasty

needs to be removed varies a lot from person to person, and not everyone will need changes to all three areas.

This can be performed as a standalone surgery, or in combination with other facial feminisation surgeries.

What it's like

Lower jaw reduction will be performed under general anaesthetic, and you will spend at least one night in hospital. Recovery tends to be longer than for other facial surgeries.

After the surgery you will have a large bandage around and under your jaw, and probably drains in your mouth. Speaking and eating will be restricted for a few days. You will need to be on a liquid diet for ten days and brush your teeth three times a day, plus use an antibacterial mouthwash, to remove bacteria and reduce the risk of infection. After surgery you may be given jaw-muscle strengthening exercises to prevent limiting any motion in your jaw.

Risks

Jaw reduction surgery is a low-risk surgery, but complications can happen. There can be numbness or prickling around the jaw, though this is usually temporary. There is also the risk that the result will be asymmetrical. The surgery can also risk fracturing your jaw or damaging your teeth. And another risk is chin ptosis, where the soft tissue of the chin droops downwards.[3]

Speak to your surgeon about the risks of the surgery, how common they are and if they can be fixed.

Consultation

When you go for a consultation with a facial surgeon, take photos of the sorts of facial features you are hoping for. This will help the surgeon understand what you want, and also help you to understand if your goals are realistic. No surgeon should promise

---

3   Lee, H.H. and Singh, M. (2022). Jaw reduction surgery. *Otolaryngologic Clinics of North America*, 55(4), 859–870. https://doi.org/10.1016/j.otc.2022.04.006

to make you look like such and such a famous person, but using pictures is often easier than trying to describe the changes in words. All surgeons are limited by the basic structure of your face, so be open to adjusting your expectations.

Computer imaging can be used to show the different amounts of change possible, to help you make a decision. Simulations of your face might be used to show you how different changes will look. Your surgeon may take photographs of you before and after the surgery for your medical records.

Whenever you make a change to any of the features of your face, the aim of the surgery should be to not just change one part but to ensure your whole face works harmoniously together.

Here is a list of suggested questions for a facial feminisation surgeon:

- How soon can I have the surgery?
- How much will it cost and what does that cover? What does it not cover?
- If there are complications and I need a follow-up operation, is that covered in the one cost?
- Will I need to stay in hospital?
- What will I look like when I come round? Will I have a lot of bandages or dressings?
- Who do I call if I am concerned about something? What hours are they open?
- When will my check-ups be?
- What can I do, other than stop smoking, to prepare?
- What can I do afterwards to promote healing?
- Where will the scars be?
- If there is a scar, what can I do to reduce it?
- Will I able to eat and talk after the surgery?

Risks
Swelling and bruising
All the surgeries will cause swelling and bruising of the face. If you have several operations at once, the swelling can look disfiguring

for the first week, but it will go down. Keeping your head elevated when you sleep and gentle walking can both help.

The worst of the swelling and bruising tends to go down in a few weeks, but the final look of the surgery can take six to eighteen months to be apparent.

Damage to the facial nerve

A rare risk is partial, permanent or temporary upper facial paralysis, if the surgeon injures the seventh nerve of the face. This is the nerve that allows you to raise your eyebrows in surprise or lower them to frown. It is possible, but difficult, to repair.

Scarring

All incisions leave scars. For facial surgery, surgeons aim to hide the scars where they won't be seen, either in the hair line or inside the mouth. But there is a risk of visible scarring.

Recovery

Whichever facial surgery you have, there are some general rules you will have to follow afterwards.

No exercise for at least two weeks, perhaps longer. If you feel your face swelling when you exercise, you need to rest for longer. Walking after surgery, though, is encouraged, as it helps reduce the swelling.

You cannot lie flat after facial surgery, and you will need to prop yourself up in bed to sleep. Your head needs to be elevated to prevent additional swelling and to help the natural swelling after surgery to go down. This could be for up to a month. You can buy soft wedge pillows to help you sleep propped up or use four stacked pillows.

To prevent infection, you will need to stop any electrolysis, hair plucking or waxing from your entire body for three months after facial surgery. This is because it is easy for infections to get in through the skin follicles and build up in any recent surgical sites.

Chewing and swallowing might be difficult after surgery because of your incisions and swelling. Your surgeon might recommend that you meet with a nutritionist to make sure you get enough nutrients.

Your face can look very swollen and bruised afterwards if you have several procedures in one go, and it can be quite frightening to look at. Lots of bloggers film their surgery journeys these days. It's not always helpful to see the results of surgery immediately afterwards because it's not a realistic depiction of the finished result. But for FFS, it can be useful to see how you might look postoperatively, so it is not a shock.

Some clinics offer treatments such as acupuncture and manual lymphatic drainage (MLD) to help reduce swelling after surgery. MLD is a light massage that helps remove fluid in the skin after surgery.

Final thing
Don't forget that facial feminisation can take a long time to finish recovering and stabilise into its finished look. Some can take a year or more to settle. Prepare yourself to be patient and let your body heal.

SONIA'S STORY
Sonia is 43. Originally from Poland, she now lives in Ireland. She talked to me about the facial feminisation surgery she'd had a year ago.

When I was 40 years old, I was working in a company with a lot of young people. I was dressing up, with pink hair and lots of piercings and looking like a teenager. Not looking forty years old, but trying to look like an over-sexualised version of myself. I didn't realise I was compensating for things. I thought, I love it, this is me. I didn't realise I was living my dream instead of just living as myself.

I had facial surgery in 2021. The surgeon did an incision across the crown of the head, behind my hairline, and then down behind my ears. He told me he would pull the skin down, take out my whole forehead, and smash it. And then he put it back. And now the brow ridge above my eyes is gone; it's nice and flat. My face has kinda moved back, so you can see my eyebrows more. And he raised those a little bit as well.

He put some stitches under the skin, running up my forehead; they were lifting my face up also but those are dissolvable. It could be a little bit more lifted but it's nice; the brow is much more open, and you can see much more of the space between the top of the eyelid and the eyebrow. The skin is healed now but I don't know if I should stand on my head.

He also removed some pieces of cartilage from my nose tip.

My cheeks look different, even though nothing happened to them. It's just proportions. I might have a hair transplant later, to fill bits in. I don't know.

Every surgery worried me a little bit. On my first surgery, the vaginoplasty, the most worrying thing for me was the anaesthesia. I'd never had surgery before, and I was a little bit worried I'd wake up mid-surgery. And when I had facial surgery, I thought, I hope he doesn't damage my face or make me less attractive. There's always a risk. And I was so worried it would affect my modelling.

I don't want to be a Barbie; I want to be as natural as possible. I thought, would I like to have big boobs and a funny nose like some other girls do? No. Because that wouldn't be me as a woman; it wouldn't feel like my face.

I didn't have any pain straight after the surgery, but over the night I was in a terrible state; I needed so many painkillers. The most annoying thing was the bandage on my nose and having lots of thick scabs on my nose. My face was all swollen, but there was no discolouration or anything. Slightly yellow, that was it. There were no big bruises.

It was hard to breathe because I couldn't breathe through my nose. They put tubes in my nose so I could breathe better, but the tubes just got stopped up with blood.

For anyone thinking of facial surgery, my advice would be don't go to a surgeon who promises you miracles, because miracles don't exist. What exists is – you have a body. And any given body can only handle so much. Some other girl might have other results to you. It's not necessarily that one result is better than the others.

You need to be conscious that your body is just the way it is; it's the body that you're born with. Cisgender women are born with their bodies and not every cisgender woman is born looking like a Barbie. Cisgender vaginas come in many different shapes and sizes; we need to realise that there isn't one correct way of being a woman. My ex-girlfriend had a very high forehead, and she was a very pretty woman. She wouldn't consider having a hair transplant, so why do I give a fuck?

7

Lower Surgery for Trans Men and Non-Binary People

For some people, genital surgery is an essential decision, while others have no interest. And other people are somewhere in between, sometimes wanting it, but managing without it. There is no right or wrong way to feel about your body; genital surgery is just one option to consider.

There are two lower surgeries for trans men and non-binary people, phalloplasty (phallo) and metoidioplasty (meta). "Lower surgery" is a general term for all of the genital surgeries for trans and non-binary people. Sometimes hysterectomy is also referred to as lower surgery. It is included here as it is often one of the stages for meta and phallo.

This chapter looks at the main differences between meta and phallo, and the complications that can occur. The aim is to give you a good sense of the pros and cons of each surgery to help you decide which, if either, would be right for you. The next two chapters, Chapter 8 and Chapter 9, look at meta and phallo in more detail.

Things to consider when thinking about lower surgery:

- the **look** you want
- the **functions** you want
- how much you can **afford**

- **how much surgery** you want to go through
- what **parts** of your body inside you that you would feel more comfortable without.

With either surgery, you should take your own general health and your financial situation into account too. Meta and phallo have long recovery times. They are often done in stages, with months in between surgeries for you to recover. It can be a slow process. Take some time to weigh up the different options.

Our genitals

Our genitals are complex structures. Genital reconstruction is challenging work for surgeons and the perfect option does not yet exist.

Here's a generalised image of a penis and vulva, and their surrounding structures, in case there are any parts mentioned here you are not familiar with. In real life, genitals come in a huge range of shapes and sizes. And the final look of your penis will depend on the anatomy you have to begin with, and what operation you choose.

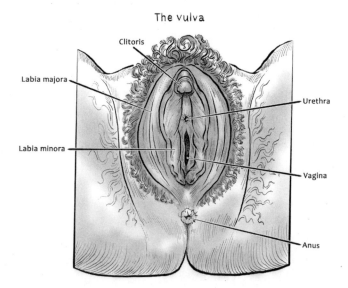

The vulva

Clitoris

Labia majora

Labia minora

Urethra

Vagina

Anus

A circumcised penis and scrotum

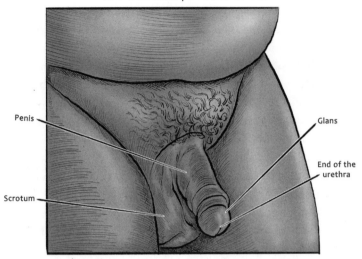

Penis

Glans

End of the
urethra

Scrotum

To get a better look at the wide variety of ways a natal penis can
look, and results from metoidioplasty and phalloplasty, visit:

- transbucket.com
- metoidioplasty.net
- phallo.net
- thebookofman.com/mind/masculinity/the-penis-gallery.

Types of lower surgery

The aims of both metoidioplasty and phalloplasty is to turn the
vulva into a penis and scrotum. This is done using the skin from
your own genitals and skin from other parts of your body. Both
surgeries are irreversible. One important difference to note is:
if you have a meta, you can later have a phallo, but not the other
way round.

Lower surgery for trans men and non-binary people includes:

- **Metoidioplasty.** A metoidioplasty uses the clitoris, which
will have grown bigger if you take testosterone, as the main
part of the new penis. The penis will be around 4 cm long.

It is then your choice if you want to have a scrotum made as well (scrotoplasty). If you choose the option to be able to pee through your penis, your urethra will be extended (urethroplasty).

- **Phalloplasty.** For phalloplasty, a large piece of skin is used to create a new penis. Five common sources for the piece of skin are the arm, thigh, belly, calf or back. A scrotum is created, and you have the option to pee through the penis or not. If you do want to pee through it, the urethra is extended down the length of the penis. You also have the option to have the penis be able to become erect or not, using an implant.

- **Vaginectomy.** Vaginectomy can be performed as part of a radical hysterectomy, or as one of the stages of metoidioplasty or phalloplasty. Removing the vagina can be performed in different ways. An excision vaginectomy involves cutting the vagina away and removing it. There are also obliterative methods, such as colpocleisis. Colpocleisis involves sewing the two sides of the vagina together, so the tube is flattened and no longer functional. Excision vaginectomy has much higher risks of complications, including haemorrhage and damage to the urinary system and bowel.

- **Scrotoplasty and testicular implants.** A scrotoplasty creates a scrotum from skin and tissue from another part of the body. This is usually done with skin from the labia majora to create the sack that testicle implants can be put in. Scrotoplasty can be done with either meta or phallo. You can choose to have testicular implants, or not. Testicular implants are silicone- or saline-filled balls used to give the shape of testicles.

- **Urethra lengthening (urethroplasty).** Your urethra is the tube that takes urine from your bladder to the hole where you pee. When a new penis is made, either as part of a meta or phallo, you have the option to be able to pee through it. Without urethra lengthening, your pee will come out where it always has, which after lower surgery will be a small hole underneath your penis. In order to extend the urethra down the length of the penis, a tube is made using skin from another part of your body. This surgery is also sometimes referred to as the "urethra hook-up".

- **Hysterectomy.** A hysterectomy removes the internal uterine reproductive organs. There are different types of hysterectomy, depending on which organs are removed (see Chapter 5: Hysterectomy). The organs that can be removed are ovaries, fallopian tubes, uterus, cervix and vagina.

To pee or not to pee from the penis

Choosing whether to pee through the new penis is an important decision when thinking about lower surgery. Most of the complications that can happen during either meta or phallo are from the urethra lengthening.

You have three options for where to pee from:

- keep your urethra where it is and keep peeing from its original location (so you would sit down to pee from an opening under the base of the penis)
- move the urethra to the base of the penis, where it can be later joined into the penis
- extend the urethra through the penis, so you pee from the tip.

Keeping it where it is has the lowest risk. You would still be able to have a scrotum created, the penis shaft and erection device, but you would just pee sitting down. You may also have the option to keep your vagina if you don't have the urethra lengthening, but not all surgeons offer this. Moving the urethra increases the risks, as there is more surgery involved.

Table of comparisons

This table contrasts the differences between metoidioplasty and phalloplasty.

	Metoidioplasty	Phalloplasty
Approximate length of new penis	Depending on your own growth, around 3–5 cm	Around 10–14 cm
How realistic does it look?	It is much smaller than the average penis; it will look more like a micropenis	It looks like a circumcised penis. Close up, its differences are clear
Can it come with scrotum and testicle implants?	Yes	Yes
Can you pee through it standing up?	Optional. Your urethra can be extended, but the penis isn't always large enough to pee outside your clothes	Optional. Your urethra can be extended
Erogenous sensation and ability to orgasm	Likely. The new penis is made from the clitoris	It depends which type of phallo you have. The clitoris will likely retain sensitivity, but it varies whether the penis shaft will be erogenous. You also have the option to have the clitoris buried under the skin or left out. Left out would have more sensitivity. More information about this in Chapter 9: Phalloplasty
Able to achieve erections	Yes. The penis is made entirely from the clitoris, so can become erect on its own	Optional, with the use of an erection device
Able to use for penetrative sex	Unlikely at the average size of 3–5 cm	Yes, with an erection device
Visible scarring after all surgeries complete	Unlikely	There is likely to be a large scar or skin graft somewhere on your body, but how visible it is when you're clothed depends on the donor site for the penis (abdomen, forearm, thigh, back or calf)

Able to keep vagina	Speak to your surgeon about your options	Speak to your surgeon about your options
Able to get pregnant after surgery	Yes, but surgeons recommend getting pregnant before meta	No
Can I deliver a baby vaginally after?	Maybe, but surgeons recommend becoming pregnant before meta	No
Reversible?	No, but you can later have phalloplasty	No
Number of surgeries involved	One to two. More if revisions are needed	Two to three, depending on what options you choose. More if you need revisions
Preparation needed	If you take hormones, six months on testosterone is recommended by the WPATH Standards of Care for the clitoris to grow. Stop smoking six weeks beforehand. If you are having the vagina removed, you will need to have a hysterectomy	Hair removal on donor site if required – this can sometimes take months. Stop smoking six weeks beforehand. If you're having the vagina removed, you will need to have a hysterectomy
Time in hospital	One to two nights. Sometimes meta is done as an outpatient surgery, meaning you can go home the same day	Different stages require different amounts of time in hospital, depending on the type of phallo you have. As a rough guide: Building the penis from the donor skin: approximately five nights; Extending the urethra: approximately two nights; Inserting the erectile device: approximately two nights
Length of recovery	Two to four weeks at each stage	Four to eight weeks at each stage

Complications

Lower surgery is a complicated process, and it is normal for there to be complications or for it to need revisions. This might be because the surgery sites aren't healing well, or because the look of the finished result isn't quite right. Sometimes small mistakes are made during surgery and the surgeon will need to repair them.

Nobody has a perfect body. Needing revisions can be disappointing, but it is better to be prepared for them than to hope everything will be perfect.

When planning your surgery timeline, give yourself space for revisions or complications (see Chapters 2, 8 and 9: Thinking About Surgery, Metoidioplasty and Phalloplasty for tips on building your timeline). This means you might need more time off work or study and more help afterwards. You might need savings to cover the impact of a second surgery or a longer recovery time. So if the recovery time says "four weeks", don't plan your wedding or holiday for five weeks after surgery; give yourself plenty of room.

Alternatives to lower surgery

Whether you're waiting for lower surgery or you've chosen not to have it, you may still be looking for ways to reduce lower body gender dysphoria. Here are a few ways people manage lower gender dysphoria:

- **Wearing a packer.** Packers are penis- and testicle-shaped objects to wear in your underwear. They give the characteristic bulge of having a penis. Some people wear them just for the look of the bulge, for example in swimming trunks. Other people find they help to reduce gender dysphoria. You can buy packers or have a go at making your own. There's more information in the following section.
- **Using different language.** If it helps you think and talk about yourself, you can use different names for your body parts. Some people call their clitoris their dick or cock, or

just their thing. The vagina is sometimes called the front hole. You can use any words that work for you.

- **Have sex or masturbate the way you want to.** Sex can trigger gender dysphoria for lots of trans and non-binary people. See Chapters 15: Sex and 16: Sexual Health and Check-Ups for ideas on ways to take part in sex while reducing gender dysphoria.

Packers

People used to make homemade packers out of a rolled-up sock or anything that gave their underwear the bulge of a penis and scrotum. It's a cheap and easy solution that still works. But you can now buy packers specially designed for trans and non-binary people.

They come in a range of sizes, including some for trans youth, a range of different skin tones and have different functions. A simple packer will be made of soft, bendy rubber and shaped like a flaccid penis with a scrotum. One side will be flat so it can sit comfortably against your body. You can tuck this straight into tight underwear, but if you wear looser underwear or want more security of it staying in place, you can wear a packer harness, packer pouch or specially designed packing underwear. The penis should be protruding from your body in the same position as where your clitoris protrudes, so you can walk and sit and ride a bike without it getting in the way.

If you are allergic to the rubber that a lot of packers are made from, you can also buy silicone packers and cloth packers.

You can also buy "stand to pee" packers, which are hollow and are shaped to fit tightly over your vulva so you can pee into them, and the pee will flow through and out the tip of the penis. These are designed to be comfortable enough to wear all day so you can use a urinal, or duck behind a tree, pee standing up, and then pop it back into your underwear. Make sure you give it a good shake to get the drips out.

Erectile packers are mid-sized and come with a bendable erection device inside. They can be worn bent down to look un-erect, and then bent up to an erect position for penetrative sex.

Packers are available from speciality companies, online sex toy shops and independent craft websites. Try searching online for "packers for trans people".

Preparing for lower surgery

For both meta and phallo, there are likely to be steps you will need to take before you can have the first stage of the surgery. Creating your own timeline of what you need to do is helpful for ensuring your surgery journey isn't delayed. There's more information in the chapters on metoidioplasty and phalloplasty (Chapters 8 and 9) on planning your surgery timeline.

Some surgeons may ask you to describe what your post-op plan is. This means having support in place to help with your recovery. Phalloplasty and metoidioplasty are both complex surgeries with several weeks of recovery time. In order for you to recover well, it's important to have people around who can support you. A post-op plan includes:

- Someone to check on you every day, if you live alone, or someone staying with you.
- Someone you can call in an emergency.
- Someone to keep you company during the day or evening.
- Someone helping you keep track of appointments, and to go with you.
- Someone to help you keep track of painkillers or other medication you're taking, and making sure you have enough.
- Someone for any additional help you'll need, such as a translator, mobility help, help with washing and drying yourself and keeping your wound sites clean and dry.

If you are not out as trans where you work or study (and there is no pressure to be), it could be useful to think of a good reason why you are taking an extended sick leave, as sometimes people ask. It is okay to just tell your manager – "I need surgery. It's personal!" Or, "I need surgery on my groin."

If you have a phalloplasty that uses the forearm as the donor site, you will always have a large area of skin on your arm that will look different, where the skin graft was taken from. You might want to have an explanation for this, as people may ask. How you manage questions – whether you want to be completely truthful, mostly truthful or completely private – is entirely your choice. There's no right or wrong answer.

If you are finding it hard to weigh up the differences between meta and phallo, have a look at the exercise in Chapter 2: Thinking About Surgery.

Final thing

If you know lower surgery is right for you, it's still important to be mentally prepared. Any surgery can take a toll on your body. Know the risks, prepare for the recovery, get as healthy as you can (it doesn't have to be perfect) and ideally, get some people around you to help you out as you recover.

JOHN'S STORY

John lives in the UK. He initially planned to get phalloplasty, but his operation was delayed when it couldn't be funded on the NHS where he lived. He talked to me about his frustration waiting for the operation and then coming to terms with his body without surgery.

By 2005, I'd had top surgery and I'd been on testosterone for a number of years; I was able to move through society as a man. I hadn't had a sexual relationship, though, and I was feeling more and more dysphoric about my genitals. At that point I would pack, and I sometimes used a homemade stand-to-pee device if I was camping, but I always felt anxious about it. Nowadays folk have professionally made packers, but back then you didn't. The most pressing issue, though, was I wanted to be able to have sex the way in my dreams I have sex, so that was probably the main thing that made me want phalloplasty.

The gender identity clinic said, "Well, it's available but don't get your hopes up for the results." And I found out via the FTM Network[1] newsletter that, at the time, the London surgical team seemed to be having a lot of complications. People were taking four or five years to get through the surgeries. I looked into what the team in Belgium was doing and I liked the sound of them better. So I got referred to both surgical teams. I went to Belgium, got approved by their psychiatrist, and got put on their waiting list, which was about three years. The London team at that point had I think about a six-month waiting list.

But as it happened, my local NHS health board wasn't prepared to fund phalloplasty anywhere, unless it fell into an "exceptional circumstance". I had to put an application in and each year they would consider whether they would fund me. For about three years they kept saying – maybe next year, but not this year.

I considered moving to another area where I could get phalloplasty funded, but I really didn't want to move. And moving felt like letting my NHS health board get away with being arseholes. So instead I started campaigning and fighting against it. While I was still fighting, I got to the top of the waiting list for Belgium, but I hadn't got the funding yet.

That was probably the most upsetting point. I definitely felt suicidal and acutely distressed when the date for the operation came through and I had to email them to say, "I can't take this due to lack of funding; you've got to give the slot to someone else." They said, "Okay, do you want to go back to the start of the waiting list, which is now four years, or be removed entirely?" And I said, "Put me back to the start again."

I just felt really hopeless then, I felt like I had fought so hard for stuff and yet I couldn't get it through at the final hurdle. With no funding, it still felt very out of reach for me. So I thought, okay, let yourself go through the stages of grief.

---

1   The FTM Network was an early online forum for trans masculine people, a space to meet people, ask questions and get support.

You have lost something that was important to you. Accept that this is necessary to process it.

The funding problem was finally resolved in 2014. I would have had to get reassessed, and again join the end of the surgery waiting list. But by that point I was actually in a relationship, and I'd found ways of coping sexually. It was still frustrating, but I felt I had already grieved for not having the phalloplasty.

Also, I'd always known about the complications that can happen during phalloplasty, but I'd assumed once you were healed there would be no more problems. But I kept hearing about people who were getting recurring urinary tract infections (UTIs) and there didn't seem to be anything that could be done.

I thought, is feeling less frustrated when I have sex worth feeling more frustrated in day-to-day life because of UTIs? Because it's really only in the middle of sex that I have to struggle to cope with things not being wired up the way I want. Most of the day I don't think about not having a penis.

And I had been able to get some psychosexual counselling. I'd always been scared of talking about it to cisgender people, but I was able to find a counsellor I could talk about my sexual frustration with. I realised there are so many ways cisgender guys can feel the same frustrations I feel. Nobody has a body that's perfect, and lots of people have issues with sex. It doesn't mean you have to be looking enviously at other folk.

So now I actually feel very comfortable with my body, and don't feel any need to make further changes. Even though at times I felt, *how can I make it through this?*, it's worked out fine.

I guess that would be my message to anyone who, for whatever reason, can't get a procedure they want – yeah, it's very distressing, but it doesn't need to destroy your life. Because there is more to your life. Even though that can feel really hard to keep hold of, when you're in the midst of a massive fuck up, there is more to your life than your transition.

8

Metoidioplasty

Metoidioplasty is a lower surgery that creates a small penis using the clitoris, as well as using skin and tissue from around the genitals to create a scrotum. This is usually only possible when the clitoris has enlarged due to taking testosterone. The amount of clitoris growth you can get from testosterone varies from person to person. The size of the new penis after metoidioplasty can also vary; it tends to be between 3 cm and 10 cm. The average is around 5 cm.

If you are googling for information on this surgery, you will find it has a few different spellings: metoidioplasty, metaidioplasty and metaoidioplasty. Often it is shortened to just "meta", which is what we'll call it here for the rest of the chapter.

There are several options for how the meta can be performed, giving you the choice to:

- pee through the new penis, or keep where you pee from
- have a scrotum created, with or without testicle implants
- keep the vagina or have the vagina removed.

The previous chapter covers the main differences between meta and phallo, and the options available for each surgery.

While most people have top surgery first and then have lower surgery, this is not required by the WPATH Standards of Care. You can have lower surgery first if you prefer.

All about the clitoris

The anatomy of the clitoris is similar to that of the penis. The clitoris and the penis develop in the uterus from the same structure: the genital tubercle. Both are erectile organs, meaning they get larger and become harder when sexually aroused.

The clitoris

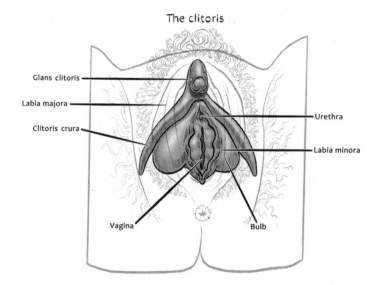

In the eighth week of human development, the external genitalia look the same, made up of just a genital tubercle, genital swellings, urethral folds and an anal fold. But then the genitals start to change.

In some people the urethral folds fuse, forming a urethra for a penis. The genital swellings become the scrotum and the genital tubercle becomes the glans penis. In other people the urethral folds remain unfused and develop into the labia minora, while the genital swellings become the labia majora and the genital tubercle becomes the clitoris.

The majority of the clitoris is inside the body, and really it's only the tip that's visible externally. Inside the body, the bulbs, crura and corpora are also made of erectile tissue. The tip is known as the glans clitoris, just like the head of the penis is known as the glans penis. The clitoris is covered by the clitoral hood, which is part of the labia minora.

Unlike the penis, the clitoris serves no other function than erogenous sensation (meaning touching it gives a sexual response), whereas the penis also contains the urethra, which pee and semen flow through.

How the surgery is done

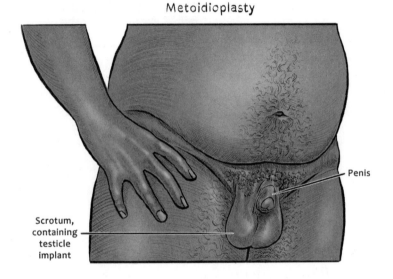

Metoidioplasty

Penis

Scrotum, containing testicle implant

Meta turns the clitoris into a penis by lengthening it and straightening it. This involves cutting two ligaments that hold the clitoris in place so that it falls forward and further out from the body. This also helps it hang a little straighter. It is a bit like the difference between a curtain that is held back with a tie and just letting the curtain fall straight down. Doing this can give you around 50 per cent more length.

The glans clitoris is then sculpted to look like the glans of a penis. If you choose to have a scrotum, this is made from the skin of the labia majora (scrotoplasty). The scrotum is the two bags of skin that hold the testicles. You can have a scrotum created with or without testicular implants. Testicular implants are usually made from silicone rubber and come in a range of sizes. Adding the testicular implants can be done at the same time, or as a second surgery.

If you want to pee through the penis, you will need to have your urethra extended (an urethroplasty) down the penis shaft. Before meta surgery, the urethra ends in a tiny hole below the clitoris and above the vagina. In a urethroplasty, the surgeon extends the urethra down the length of the new penis by creating a small tube from hairless skin from another part of your body. This is often from the skin lining the insides of your cheek (the buccal mucosa) or skin from the labia minora. After the urethra has been created, the surgeon will leave a small plastic tube inside it (called a stent) to prevent it from closing up while it heals. During this time you will have a catheter coming out directly from your bladder through your lower belly. This is a suprapubic catheter. It will drain urine into a bag, which you will have to empty throughout the day. The stent will be kept in for around ten days and the catheter for two to three weeks.

The surgery typically takes around two to five hours, and you may stay in hospital for a day or two, depending on what options you went for, and how you are healing. Depending on what you choose, and what your surgeon offers, you may also be able to have a hysterectomy at the same time.

You also have the choice to keep your vagina or have it removed and the vaginal opening closed at the same time as the meta. Check with your surgeon if they perform meta this way.

The technique for performing the meta can vary from surgeon to surgeon. You might hear the terms simple metoidioplasty, ring metoidioplasty and extensive metoidioplasty. These are all different variations. If you are keen to know more details about how your surgery will be performed, be sure to ask your surgeon, or look up free surgical articles on sites such as scholar.google.com.

You may be advised to have other surgeries to improve the outcome of lower surgery, such as a majora fold reduction or a monsplasty. A majora fold reduction removes some of the tissue of the labia majora. A monsplasty removes some of the fatty tissue of the mons pubis, in order for the new penis to stand further out.

Preparing for surgery

Before the surgery you will either be invited to a consultation with the surgeon or you will book one yourself. The consultation is a chance to ask questions about the surgery and check how your own health and circumstances might be impacted. Below is a suggested list of questions to ask. There is a space at the end of the book to add your own notes and questions.

- How do you perform the surgery?
- When can I have the surgery? Can I pick a time that suits me a bit better?
- Do I need to do any preparation, such as stop smoking or anything else?
- Do I need to stop taking testosterone?
- How long will I be in hospital?
- What are the common complications? How are they resolved?
- What will it be like when I wake up? Will I be able to sit or just lie down?
- How long will I be off work? (And let them know if you have a physically demanding job.)
- How long until I can start swimming/running/cycling/weightlifting etc.?
- How long until I can have sex or masturbate?
- If I have complications when I'm home, who do I contact?
- I will need a sick note for work or study; where do I get this from?
- How much is the surgery and what does that cost cover? Does it cover fixing any complications? (If you will be paying for surgery yourself.)

If you are a smoker, or you use nicotine products of any kind, including gum, patches, vaping or e-cigarettes, it is very likely the surgeon will require you to stop using them six weeks before the surgery and continue to not use them afterwards for several weeks. Some surgeons may also ask you to stop taking testosterone several weeks before the surgery, to reduce the risk of deep vein thrombosis.

You might be asked to "pump up" the clitoris in preparation for surgery. Options might include using a pump device or applying dihydrotestosterone directly to the clitoris. You can use the pump device without supervision, but do not apply testosterone to your clitoris without a doctor's support.

Clitoris pumps are made by a range of brands and come in different shapes and sizes. They can be bought online, often from sex toy shops.

Even if you are not planning on having surgery, some people like to use "pumping" to give their genitals more length and girth. This can work well but it is usually temporary, and your genitals may return to their normal size unless you pump regularly.

When you're pumping start slow, and don't pump for too long. Start with the smallest size "cup", and use plenty of lube in the cup so your genitals don't get stuck!

Timeline

It is useful to plan out your timeline of the things you need to do, the order they need to be done in and how long they will take. This helps you see in advance when steps are likely to fall, in case you need to avoid anything clashing with something important, like an exam or religious festival. Some steps may happen simultaneously. For meta, the steps you need to take are:

- Get one letter of referral for hysterectomy (if you're having it).
- Get one letter of referral for metoidioplasty.
- Have the hysterectomy and recover.
- Give your body a rest period after recovery from hysto before having the first stage of meta (around three months).
- Be on a waiting list for metoidioplasty (check how long this is when you go for a consultation).

Meta surgery, depending on what options you want, can happen over a few surgeries, with waiting times in between for you to recover from each stage. Sometimes, if you have complications, you may need extra surgery.

Each stage will involve a considerable recovery time, meaning four to eight weeks off from work, studying or doing your everyday tasks. The timeline could look something like what is outlined below.

Timeline for going through metoidioplasty

Surgical steps	Simultaneous steps	Your personal timeline
Six months of testosterone is recommended, if you choose to take testosterone	Prepare fertility options if you want to freeze your eggs	
Get referred for hysterectomy and meta		
Go for a consultation for meta and confirm what options you want		
Have the hysterectomy and recover before Stage 1 of the meta (six-month break)		
Have Stage 1 of the meta, and fully recover		
After recovery, wait three to six months before booking Stage 2		
Have Stage 2 of the meta (if required) and fully recover		

Going into hospital

While you're in hospital, you might want to make sure you have clothes with you that will be comfortable for resting and that are easy to get in and out of. It's a good idea to have loose clothing, such as baggy pyjamas or large shorts, for your lower half that won't put pressure on your groin and has space for bandages.

You may have some bleeding in the first week or two after the surgery, so if you have furniture, bedding or a mattress that you don't want to risk getting any blood on, get a few cheap, dark-coloured towels so you can cover where you are sitting or sleeping. You could get a plastic mattress cover also.

Here's a suggested shopping list:

- dark towels for the sofa or bed
- baggy pyjamas, shorts and underwear
- period or continence pads – very useful for absorbing blood if you have some extra bleeding
- moist toilet paper – useful for helping keep your bum clean when wiping delicately around stitches and swollen areas
- a few flannels for washing at the sink rather than a bath or shower.

Being in hospital

For metoidioplasty you'll probably be in hospital only one or two nights, but it's still worth planning ahead how you'll spend your time. Have a look at Chapter 12: Preparing for Surgery to make sure you have ways to kill time and stay distracted.

Leaving hospital

Healing from metoidioplasty can take some time, and how long it takes varies from person to person. Your surgeon and nurses can give you guidance, but it's important to listen to your own body too and give yourself more time if you need it.

It is usually recommended to do only light activity for the

first week or so (e.g. pottering around the house, making a small meal). Your surgeon will advise you on how and when you can shower, but be prepared to go a few days without showering or bathing to avoid getting your stitches wet. You may be washing at the sink, so it's handy to have a flannel if you don't have one.

You shouldn't do strenuous activity or heavy lifting, such as lifting heavy objects (including animals and children!), working out, running or carrying heavy shopping, for around six weeks after surgery.

Peeing through your penis

If you have had a urethra extension to be able to pee through the penis, you will wear a stent (a narrow plastic tube) in the penis for approximately the first ten days, and a suprapubic catheter will be coming out of your belly to drain urine. This is to prevent the new urethra from closing up.

Having a suprapubic catheter in place shouldn't be painful. If you experience any redness or pain around the area where the tube comes out, or see blood in your urine, contact your doctor.

When you have the catheter removed and pee for the first time through the new penis, you may find it sprays all over the place. Try peeing for the first time in the shower or bath, in case it comes out sideways or goes in all directions. This is normal and usually settles down in time.

Common complications

You may be asked to use a pump or a phosphodiesterase type-5 inhibitor (the vasodilators used for erectile dysfunction) after surgery to prevent your new penis retracting.

Most of the complications after meta are related to creating the urethra. Some are minor and resolve themselves. Some require surgical intervention. The minor complications are:

• dribbling or spraying after peeing

- haematoma (bleeding under the skin)
- infection
- partial skin necrosis (when part of the skin dies and needs to be removed).

There are two more serious complications with metoidioplasty. These are fistulae (when a hole between two parts of the body opens up) and stricture (when a passage through the body seals up). Sometimes fistulae repair themselves, but either of these may require surgical repair.

Another complication is rejection of the testicular implants. When implants are displaced or rejected, the surgeon will remove them and replant them three to six months later.

Erogenous sensation and sex

After meta surgery, erogenous sensation may be different at first. There are a lot of nerves in the genitals, and they may be affected by the surgery and how the tissues have been moved around. This can take a while to recover, but it is likely to correct itself with time.

In order to let your new penis heal and recover, it's advised to leave it alone for a few weeks. It might be tempting to masturbate out of curiosity, boredom or frustration. While the guidance for recovery tends to focus on physical activity and stress, rubbing and poking around in the area that has just been stitched together is probably best left alone until it's well healed.

Final thing

If you have kept your vagina, cervix, ovaries or uterus, it's important to know how to keep them healthy. If you do have a cervix, and you have sexual contact with someone of any gender, you should go for regular smear tests. See Chapter 16: Sexual Health and Check-Ups for more information.

BRYN'S STORY

Bryn, 48, has been going through the stages of metoidioplasty over the last eight years. He'd had three stages, and one extra stage to fix complications, when we met up to talk.

It took me years to come to the decision. I knew I didn't want a phalloplasty, partly because I don't care about size, and partly because my job is all about using my hands so I wasn't prepared to risk my career having the forearm graft method.[1]

A lot of what helped me decide was seeing a friend go through the different stages. If you've got someone who's happy to show you what they've got, that really does help.

Physically, one of the things I liked about meta was the ability to still get an erection. Peeing standing up I wasn't sure about until I was in the consultation, and then he asked and I said yes and knew it was the right answer.

I packed for a while, mostly in the early stages of transition. It was one of those extra cues that people look at. And then I did a photo shoot for a naked calendar, like a "calendar girls" calendar, but with all trans men. And the group photo shoot for December was the first time I saw people whose bodies mirrored mine. No one had had lower surgery. It was really liberating. I pretty much stopped packing from then on.

At the consultation I wrote out all my questions for the surgeon because I knew that as soon as I got there my brain would fall out, and I'd forget everything. I also took my partner with me. If you've got somebody else there, they'll probably remember a different bit than you did. Ask the surgeon if you can record it. And get the other person to take notes, so you can ask all the questions and just listen when the surgeon is talking to you.

The surgeon did talk about pumping after the first stage, but to be careful because it can damage the tissues. I think it's quite helpful for making sure things don't retract. I did a

---

1   The forearm method involves removing one of the nerves in the arm so it can be used in the penis. Bryn works with his hands and was concerned this could lead to some loss of sensitivity in his hand.

lot of pumping of the scrotum to stretch that, and I think that helped. With actually pumping the penis, it gives a short-term increase if you keep doing it regularly, but within a week of stopping it shrinks back to what it was before so I can't be arsed.

Recovery

I like to be left alone when I'm ill; I don't want people there. Though one thing that was nice was, on the third stage, there was someone in the hospital who was having the same stuff done, and we spent the whole evening in my room chatting. That was lovely. Even if you don't see anyone in hospital, if you know there are other people going through stuff at the same time, it helps.

Then I had an extra stage after the second stage. Because they'd done it in a slightly different way to some people's and because I'd had a massive hematoma that had distorted everything as it was healing, the shaft of my penis was turned by about 45 degrees. So instead of my pee hole being forward and down, mine was pointing at about four o'clock. Plus, they needed to move my scrotum a bit; there wasn't enough of a bag. And the end of the head had split so my pee hole was open more than it should have been. Any one of those things they could have done at the next stage, but because it was all three they decided to do it as a separate stage.

I had a hematoma with every stage. One of them was in the scrotum. I got up in the night because I was in pain, and the hematoma just went splat on the bathroom floor. So then I had a hole, but it just healed itself from inside. Took about ten days and then it was just completely gone.

Peeing, to start with, was chaotic because there was a lot of swelling in the tube. It was very much on sprinkler setting to start with. But once it settled down it was so satisfying to have a pee outside and not have to worry about getting nettles on my bum or peeing on my shoes. At home I don't tend to pee standing up because it's a bit drippy. It's short enough that it's hard to angle.

Psychologically, I went for meta because I just wanted to feel more comfortable and not at odds with my own body. I didn't have massively dysphoric feelings, but I wanted my physical body to fit the body map that my brain has. Now, I feel fine. Even though the penis on my body map before was bigger than I have now, that's reset and fitted to the size I have now. I don't feel my body doesn't match anymore.

9

Phalloplasty

The aim of phalloplasty surgery is to create a penis that can be used for peeing, can get erect enough for penetrative sex, feels erogenous (creates a sexual response) and looks realistic. You have some options with how the new penis is created and what it can do.

In this chapter we're going to refer to the type of penis created from a phalloplasty as a penis or "new penis", and the type someone is born with as a "natal penis", to be able to talk about the differences.

This chapter aims to give you an overview of the range of options available for phalloplasty surgery, and the limitations of the surgery.

Phalloplasty is a complicated surgery and there is no agreed-upon method by all surgeons. There are a number of options for how the result can be achieved, and each surgical team that performs it may use a slightly different method.

There are a lot of different things to weigh up when considering phalloplasty. But one of the most important is to be sure this is the surgery you want. Even if you are certain that your dysphoria would be greatly relieved if you could change your genitals to match your gender, consider if the outcomes of phalloplasty are what you want. Put another way, even if you know you want a penis, be sure that you want a phalloplasty.

There are photo galleries online that you can browse to get a sense of the range of results different phalloplasty techniques produce. It is hard to know exactly how it will feel, as everyone is different.

Phalloplasty is done over a series of surgeries, and there is quite a bit of information to take in and options to consider. It can get overwhelming. If this is the surgery for you, take your time digesting the information. Use the spaces at the end of the book to list all the questions that come up for you. It might be useful to keep a notebook, or a file on your phone, to make a note of questions or ideas that you think of when you're doing other things.

Phalloplasty is not one procedure; it is a range of procedures that can be combined to meet each person's goals. But while the new penis can function and look quite realistic, it is unlikely to look and feel exactly like a natal penis.

I only thought I wanted it because I thought I ought to. I guess I thought to be a fully correct trans man I have to go through all of these exact steps. But the delay [between the first and second stage] has given me time to really settle into who I actually am as a person and nail down what I want from my transition and how my sexual orientation factors into that.

Jack

What is the penis like?

Phalloplasty creates a new penis and scrotum that can have four key features:

- You can pee through the new penis, including standing to pee at urinals (or in the woods in an emergency).
- The new penis can get hard and be used for penetrative sex with the use of an erection device (more on how later).
- It can become erogenous and can be used to orgasm.
- It looks pretty much like a circumcised penis with a scrotum, both inside and outside clothing. Up close, it's possible to see differences. But it's unlikely people will

be paying enough attention to tell the difference during a quick change at the swimming baths or standing at a urinal.

- It is a similar size to the average adult natal penis. The new penis is the same length when flaccid and erect, usually around 10 to 14 cm. The average size for an erect adult natal penis is between 13 and 15 cm.

How is it different from a natal penis?

- It can't get hard on its own.
- It doesn't come in a huge range of sizes. The length and girth you get is dependent on the donor site (where the skin is taken from to make the penis). You're likely to get something between 10 to 14 cm.
- It doesn't have the layers of skin that move on the shaft that a natal penis does. The overall feel is different to a natal penis because of the tissue it is made of.
- It won't necessarily be as erogenous as a natal penis. If you use a method that allows the new penis to be erogenous, most people get good sensitivity and are able to orgasm. But this can take a little time to fully take effect, and it might not be as sensitive as you would like, or as sensitive as a clitoris. Some of the donor site options don't allow it to be erogenous, but you are still able to orgasm using your clitoris.

If the phalloplasty you have includes removing the vagina, you will need to have a hysterectomy beforehand. The hysterectomy is to remove the cervix and the uterus. Without a vagina, the cervix and uterus can no longer be accessed to check for cancer and therefore need to be removed too.

Standing to pee and penetrative sex are possible whichever donor site is used for the surgery. However, depending on which donor site is used, erogenous sensation can vary.

GENDER CONFIRMATION SURGERY

How this surgery is done

Unlike metoidioplasty, phalloplasty is usually done in two or more stages. This is because phalloplasty involves a lot of procedures, and breaking it up allows the body to heal and recover before the next stage. Surgeons recommend leaving at least three months between stages.

While they may be combined in slightly different ways, the stages of phalloplasty are:

Stage 1

Create the new penis. Creating a penis involves taking a large piece of skin from another part of the body and rolling it into a tube to create the basic penis shape. The large piece of skin is often called a "flap". This tube is then sewn onto the groin. Blood vessels and nerves from the groin are joined to the blood vessels and nerves in the new penis. In some cases, a piece of skin is taken from another part of the body to cover the area where the first flap was taken.

Stage 2

Urethroplasty, scrotoplasty and clitoral burial. Whichever donor site you are interested in, you will have the option to have the urethra lengthened so you can pee through the new penis (urethroplasty). If you have the urethra lengthened, it's often done as a second stage, before the erection device. The surgeons will use skin from the vagina, forearm, labia minora or sometimes from the inside of the cheek to create a tube that extends from the bladder to the tip of the penis. While the urethroplasty heals, you may have a suprapubic catheter for around two to three weeks. This is a tube that comes directly from your bladder out through your lower stomach to a bag attached to your leg. Urine will drain directly into the bag throughout the day, which you can empty into a toilet by turning a valve. The second stage can also include the labia minora and majora being reshaped into a scrotum for testicle implants. The clitoris can be buried under the skin or left out. The head of the penis will be sculpted into the shape of a glans, to look like a circumcised penis.

Stage 3

Erection device and testicular implants. Whichever donor site is used for the surgery, you will have the option to have an erection device implanted. If you are choosing to have an erection device, this is usually done as a final stage. There are two types of erection device – there's more information about these later in the chapter.

The donor sites

There are five sites on the body usually used for the donor "flap". This piece of skin needs to be quite large in order to make a new penis that is around 10 to 14 cm long and wide enough to have the girth of an average penis.

Each donor site has different pros and cons, and not every site is suitable for everyone. Some only work if there is not a lot of body fat under skin. Scarring on the area also might make the location unsuitable because scars can limit the blood supply to an area of skin. This would be something to discuss with your surgeon at the consultation, as scarring is very varied. Also, not every surgeon performs every type of phalloplasty.

Tattoos don't typically prevent you from using the skin as a donor site, though of course it will lead to a tattooed penis, and a gap in the tattoo where the flap was removed from.

The five common sites on the body used for the donor flap are:

- the abdomen
- the forearm
- the thigh
- the back
- the calf.

Erogenous sensation

As part of the phalloplasty you have the option to have your clitoris "buried" or left exposed. If it is buried, it will lie under the skin below the base of the new penis. It will still be sexually sensitive, but the feeling is likely to not be as acute because of the layer of skin over it. If it is left exposed, it will be visible under the base of the penis.

You also have the option to have a "nerve hook-up" for some of the phalloplasty methods. When the donor flap of skin is taken, it will contain a good nerve that is used so you can feel sensation in the new penis, like hot and cold and pressure. But in order to have erogenous sensation in the penis, the nerve needs to be attached to the nervous system of the clitoris. This way, the erogenous sensation of the clitoris is transferred into the penis.

The clitoris has two major nerves that give it erogenous sensation. Surgeons will join one of these to the nerve of the new penis and leave the other attached to the clitoris. This way, the new penis can become erogenous but if the nerve hook-up fails, the clitoris will still retain its sensation and ability to orgasm.

The new penis, even when the nerve hook-up is entirely successful, is unlikely to be as sensitive as the clitoris. How sensitive it is depends on the donor site. Also, it won't be fully sensitive straight away. It takes six months or more for the nerves to heal and start to give full sensitivity.

Not all phallo methods can use the nerve hook-up. We have different types of nerves in our body for different functions. Basically, motor nerves deliver messages from the brain that do things like make muscles move. Sensory neurons respond to the environment and tell us if something is, for example, hot or cold. There is a lot more complexity to it than just that, of course, but the important thing to know for phalloplasty is that a sensory nerve can't deliver motor messages, and a motor nerve can't deliver sensory messages.

One last thing: sexual pleasure isn't the same for everyone. Some people don't experience sexual desire and have little or no interest in sex. They might identify as asexual. Being asexual is not a sign that something is wrong, nor is it something someone should "get over"; it is on the spectrum of sexuality just like everything else. Some trans and non-binary people are asexual, but this doesn't mean they wouldn't want lower surgery.

The abdomen

For this method, the new penis is created from skin and tissue from your stomach. The surgeon will take a rectangle of skin above the pubic area and first fold it down, so it hangs down where a penis sits, then fold it into a tube.

Donor site on the abdomen

The area across your stomach where the flap was taken is then pulled together and sewn, so a skin graft from another part of the body is not required. This is possible because the skin of your stomach is stretchy. It leaves a thin, wide scar across your lower abdomen that curves up at each end. It also leaves a scar along the top of the penis, where the two sides of the flap join.

This type of flap is called a pedicled flap. It is not entirely removed from the body during the surgery and retains its blood supply throughout. Whenever a flap is removed entirely from the body and grafted back on, there is a risk that the blood supply will not be 100 per cent successful and some of the tissue may die and need to be removed. The risk of this is much less with a pedicled flap.

The disadvantage of this donor site is there is not a suitable nerve in the flap to connect to the clitoris. So while the clitoris will retain erotic sensitivity, the penis will not have the same sensitivity. It will feel hot and cold and pressure but not give an erogenous sensation when touched. Another disadvantage is the scar that runs along the top of the penis. This will fade with time, though, and can be further disguised with medical tattooing.

The forearm

This method is known as the radial forearm phalloplasty or radial forearm free flap because it takes skin that includes the radial artery from the forearm. For this method, the donor site is a rectangular piece of skin and tissue from around the forearm. This is then rolled into a "tube within a tube" shape and used as both the urethra and penis. If you choose not to have your urethra extended, the rectangle will be smaller.

The forearm is then covered with a split-thickness graft or acellular dermal matrices (a type of surgical mesh) and a skin graft later. Tissue from another part of the body is taken to graft over the donor site. For example, it may be taken from the buttocks, where two strips of tissue can be taken and the two sides of the incision can be pulled together, because the skin is very stretchy on the buttocks.

Donor site on the forearm

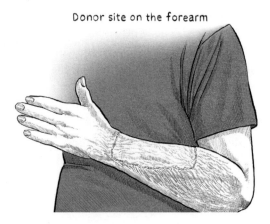

This surgery uses a free flap, meaning the flap is lifted away entirely from one part of the body and reattached to another part. There is a greater risk of tissue loss with this type of flap; it depends how well the blood vessels join up.

The advantages of the forearm donor site are a large nerve in the flap that gives a good chance of sensation developing in the penis, and a good aesthetic result.

The disadvantages are the large skin graft on the forearm is visible any time you wear short sleeves. It can be disguised somewhat with a tattoo, depending on how it heals.

The thigh

For this method, a free or pedicled flap can be taken from the top of the thigh. It is known as the anterolateral thigh phalloplasty or ALT phalloplasty. The rectangular flap is a full-thickness flap, meaning all the tissue down to the muscle is taken from the thigh, rolled into a tube and grafted onto the groin. Then a piece of skin is taken from the other thigh and grafted over the area where the main flap was taken.

The area where the flap was taken from will be left with a large, visible skin graft scar, and the other thigh will have a much fainter scar. Usually this is barely visible after a few years.

The advantage of the thigh as a donor site is the large skin graft is easier to conceal in day-to-day life than a skin graft on the forearm.

Donor site on the thigh

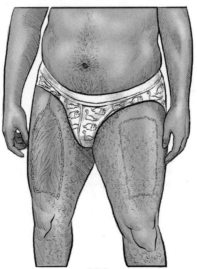

The tissue from the donor site can sometimes be bulky enough to allow for penetration during sex without an erection device. Sometimes, though, the new penis can come out too bulky, and will need to be thinned down a little by a process called "debulking".

The back (not currently performed in the UK)

For this method, the donor flap is taken from the back, near the shoulder blade. This method is sometimes called the latissimus dorsi flap (LDF), or the musculocutaneous latissimus dorsi flap or myocutaneous latissimus dorsi flap (MLDF).

The latissimus dorsi is a large, triangular back muscle. The flap is taken from your non-dominant side. So if you are left handed, it will be taken from your right side. The flap is rolled into a tube and attached to the groin. But this type of flap is too bulky to be rolled around itself twice to create the "tube within a tube". Therefore, if you are choosing to have urethroplasty, the urethra will have to come from a different part of the body.

Donor site on the back

The area where the donor flap was taken from can usually be sewn up without needing a skin graft, but sometimes an extra graft is needed. It leaves a long, branched scar across the back.

This method can be done in two ways. The first uses just skin and tissue from the back to create the penis, like the other methods. This is a free flap. The second uses skin and a small piece of muscle from the back to create the penis; this is called a functional flap.

In the free flap, one of the nerves from the back can be used to create a nerve hook-up with the clitoris. However, sensation rates are generally not very good.

In the functional flap method, a motor nerve in the muscle is reattached at the groin, and some patients are able to contract the muscle in the penis. By contracting the muscle they make the penis firmer, shorter and wider, sometimes called a paradox erection. This can sometimes be used for penetrative sex without the need of an erection device, but the results are varied.

For either the free flap or functional flap method, the clitoris can be kept buried under the skin and retain good sensitivity.

The advantages of this method are there is slightly more choice of penis size, plus the long scar is fairly easy to hide in day-to-day life.

The main disadvantage, though, is the low rates of erogenous sensation in the penis itself.

The calf (not currently performed in the UK)
This method involves taking a flap of skin from the outside of the calf, plus a piece of fibula bone from inside the calf. There are two bones in the calf that run from the knee to the ankle: the fibula and tibia. The fibula is the narrower bone. This piece of bone is used to create a stable structure that is strong enough for penetrative sex without needing an erection device.

If you choose to have the urethra lengthened as part of this surgery, some surgeons will create the urethra first. The new urethra is built on your calf and allowed to heal before moving the large flap of skin, now containing the urethra, onto your groin.

This is done by taking a piece of hairless skin from another part of the body and wrapping it around a catheter. This creates the urethra. This urethra, wrapped around the tube, is placed under the skin of the calf. This can be done around six months prior to the operation to create the penis.

Donor site from the calf, including the fibula bone

Fibula

Part of the fibula has been removed

The penis is then created by opening up the leg down to the bone and removing a piece of fibula, leaving a few centimetres of bone at either end, near the ankle and the knee, to help those joints stay stable.

The flap of skin from the calf, with the new urethra attached, is then wrapped around the bone and transferred to the groin, and the piece of fibula is attached to the pelvic bone. The area on the calf is covered with a full-thickness skin graft from another part of the body. Around two to three months after the new penis has been created, the urethra will be connected up.

The advantages of the calf as a donor site are that the skin graft can be more easily hidden in everyday life by trousers or socks. Plus, using the calf bone gives it a natural rigidity.

However, having a permanent erection, as well as a piece of bone in the penis, can cause discomfort.

The nerve hook-up is possible with the calf method, but sensation in the new penis is often reported as poor (but not in the clitoris itself, which still is sensitive and buried just under the skin).

It is very likely that the skin of the leg and foot of the donor leg will have less sensation after surgery, because one of the nerves was removed to use in the penis.

The perfect method for phalloplasty has not been created yet, and it's likely all these methods will continue to be refined and adapted to improve the look and function of the penis and to reduce the complication rates. There are other methods that have been used for phalloplasty in the past but are less common now, including the groin flap, the forearm flap with a piece of radius bone and the calf flap without the bone.

But note: surgeons generally do not perform all the different types of phalloplasty. Some are more commonly performed than others. So discussing which phalloplasty technique your surgeon has experience of doing is important.

Other surgical methods used in phalloplasty
Skin expanders
Some surgeons use pre-expanders under the skin as part of the phalloplasty procedure. A pre-expander is a deflated balloon that is placed under the skin. Water is slowly added to the balloon over weeks or months, causing it to expand. This stretches the skin and causes new skin growth.

The aim is to create enough new skin to be able to cover the area where the donor flap is taken without needing a graft. Or, for the abdomen method, it helps to pull the two sides of the area together more easily. This allows the abdomen method to be used for thinner people who might not have enough skin elasticity otherwise. Pre-expansion has high rates of complications at the moment though (52 per cent of people had complications in one study).[1]

Combination of donor sites

Sometimes a combination of donor sites might be used. For example, using the thigh and the arm. This would be a way to minimise the size of the skin graft on the arm. It might also be suitable for a patient with very thin arms, or thigh skin that wasn't suitable for both flaps.

Preparing for surgery

See Chapter 7: Lower Surgery for Trans Men and Non-Binary People for lots of general information on how to prepare for lower surgery, plus Chapter 12: Preparing for Surgery has information on generally preparing for a surgery. There are some good tips there on keeping yourself entertained while you're recovering and making sure you have the support you need. Plus there's a checklist of key tasks to get done before you go into hospital.

For phalloplasty, though, there are a few things to emphasise. Phalloplasty is a bigger surgery than metoidioplasty, especially the first stage when the penis itself is created. Preparing for recovery involves pretty much the same stages as the other surgeries, but the recovery may take longer.

The first stage of phallo usually involves taking the donor flap and grafting it to the groin. This requires a stay in hospital for around five to seven days, and the first two days after surgery you may be advised to stay in bed and not move. Keeping yourself calm and entertained is key.

Hair removal

If you are choosing to have urethroplasty, the skin used for the

---

1   Elfering, L., *et al.* (2019). Preexpansion in phalloplasty patients: Is it effective? *Annals of Plastic Surgery, 83*(6), 687–692. https://doi.org/10.1097/SAP.0000000000001968

urethra needs to be entirely hairless. Some of the phallo methods use the "tube within a tube" technique. This method uses one piece of skin to create both the urethra and the penis. These methods often need hair removal from the part of the skin that will be used for the tube for the urethra. This is because any hair inside the urethra can cause infection and blockages, and it is impossible to remove the hair once the urethra is finished.

Other methods for creating the urethra, such as using the inside of the cheek or pieces of vaginal tissue, do not require any hair removal. This is because these parts of the body are naturally hairless.

Unless you want a hairy new penis, you will need to have the hair permanently removed from the skin used for the outside of the new penis as well, using electrolysis. But hair removal on the outside of the penis can also be performed after the phalloplasty.

Electrolysis is a lengthy process. To remove the hair just from the urethra donor site will take several sessions and could take a few months. It will depend on how often you are available to go and how much you can afford each month.

Timeline

Phalloplasty surgery, depending on what combination of options you want, can take up to three separate surgeries, with waiting times in between for you to recover from each stage. Sometimes, if you have complications, you may need extra surgery.

There is no agreed-upon order that the stages of phalloplasty have to be done in, so you will find surgeons vary in how they perform the steps.

Each stage will involve a considerable recovery time, meaning four to eight weeks off from work, studying or doing your everyday tasks. The timeline could look something like this:

Timeline for going through phalloplasty

Surgical steps	Simultaneous steps	Your personal timeline
	Prepare fertility options if you want to freeze your eggs	
Get referred for hysterectomy and phalloplasty		
Go for a consultation for phalloplasty and confirm whether you need to have hair removal	Begin hair removal if required. Depending on the donor site, cost and your availability, this could be a few months to a year of treatment	
Have the hysterectomy and recover before Stage 1 of the phallo (six-month break)		
Have Stage 1 of the phalloplasty, and fully recover		
After recovery, wait three to six months before booking Stage 2		
Have Stage 2 of the phalloplasty and fully recover		
After recovery, wait three to six months before Stage 3, if you're having it		
Have Stage 3 of phalloplasty, depending on which method you have, and fully recover		

So it could easily be around two to three years or more to go through the whole process. It is time consuming and it can be frustrating to wait. Other life events can come along that also interrupt your progress.

Going home from hospital

Whatever method you have, recovery at home can be difficult with phalloplasty. You will probably need help with a lot of things such as cooking, shopping, dressing, washing, moving in and out of bed or just having things brought to you so you don't have to move around a lot.

When you come out of hospital after the new penis has been attached, you will need to keep it in a position sticking straight out from your body for a few weeks. This is partly because the stitches at the base attaching it to your body are not strong enough to support its weight. It is also to prevent the penis from kinking as it hangs down, which would restrict the blood flow.

This means you will have what looks like a permanent erection, plus bulky bandages in your groin, for a few weeks. So consider clothing you might need to protect the penis and not put pressure on it or the bandages as the stitches heal, such as loose nightshirts or dressing gowns.

As your recovery for this stage comes to an end, you may find you need larger underwear after your surgery, as you have a new bit of body to fit in them now.

Erection devices

There are two different types of erection devices. Ask your surgeon about which they use and why. If you have a preference, this would be important to discuss with your surgeon.

Pump erection devices

Pump erection devices are made of three parts: rods that sit in the shaft of the penis, a ball-shaped pump that sits in the scrotum and a reservoir of fluid that sits in the abdomen. When you squeeze the pump three or four times, fluid from the reservoir fills the rods in the shaft. These swell, imitating the effect of blood filling the vessels of a natal penis. The new penis becomes firmer and rises to stick out from the body.

When you want the erection to go away, a small button on the side of the pump releases the fluid back into the reservoir and the penis becomes limp. It takes four or five seconds to become hard, and about the same to go limp.

The back of the rods are fixed to the pubic bone, to ensure the penis, rods and your body all move in synchronicity. This is especially important during penetrative sex.

The advantage of the pump device is it closely mimics the action of a natal penis and can move quickly between soft and hard states. Plus, there is less pressure on the skin when the rods are in their soft state, which reduces the risk of the device pushing through the skin from inside and breaking through. The disadvantages are that, with more parts than the bendy devices, there is a higher risk of infection. Plus, as it is mechanical, the device doesn't last forever. Around 30 per cent need to be replaced within ten years.[2]

Pump erection device

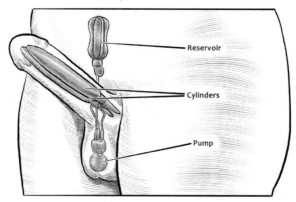

2   Andrology (2023). Penile Prosthesis. www.andrology.co.uk/phalloplasty/penile-prosthesis

Bendy erection devices

Bendy or malleable erection devices are made from silicone and steel and are fairly indestructible. They are both rigid and flexible all the time, so they are bent upwards when you want them erect and then bent down when you want them pointing down.

The disadvantage of the bendy devices is they put a constant pressure on the skin inside the penis, which can lead to them pushing through the skin to the surface. Plus the constant rigidity can be uncomfortable. Infection is also still a risk with the bendy devices.

Other options

If you can't have or choose not to have an erection device implanted, there are devices such as the Stays-Hard, which works similarly to a leg brace, fitting over your penis. You could also try a rigid condom or penile sheaf. These are bendy plastic condoms that are sometimes firm enough to allow you to have penetrative sex. With a thick cover, though, they won't give much, if any, stimulation to your penis.

Peeing standing up

If you've had the urethra lengthened, peeing standing up for the first time can be exciting or daunting or just a bit messy.

When you pee through the penis for the first time it might spray in all directions, or it might come out sideways rather than forward. This usually doesn't last. But the first time you pee, you could try doing it in the bath in case urine goes everywhere.

Many people find some pee can get trapped in the urethra and then dribble out into their underwear after they have left the toilet and carried on moving around. It is usually only a small amount, but it can be enough that it might be visible through your clothes. This is due to how the urethra is constructed; often there is a little "U-bend" created inadvertently and pee can get stuck in it, then dribble out as you move. The new penis is made from skin and fat and so doesn't have the musculature of a natal penis to prevent dribbling.

A tip to deal with this is after you've finished peeing, let the penis hang straight down and run your finger tight against the underside and along to help "scoop" out any that is left in the U-bend.

If you don't do this, the pee can wash back into your bladder and this can risk a urinary tract infection (UTI). Also, if pee dribbles into your underwear regularly it can lead to a rash, similar to nappy rash, from having your skin against the damp material.

Urinary tract infections can affect the whole urinary tract, including your bladder, urethra or kidneys. UTIs may be treated with antibiotics, but they're not always needed.

Symptoms of a UTI may include:

- pain or a burning sensation when peeing
- needing to pee more often than usual during the night
- needing to pee more often than usual during the day
- pee that looks cloudy
- needing to pee suddenly or more urgently than usual
- blood in your pee
- lower tummy pain or pain in your back, just under the ribs
- a high temperature, or feeling hot and shivery
- a low temperature below 36°.

If you think you may have a UTI, it is best to get it checked out as you may need antibiotics to clear it up. Visit your GP or a health clinic. You'll need to give a urine sample when you get there.

Complications

Complications are common with phalloplasty. Being aware of the sorts of complications that can come up helps you deal with them if they happen, whereas expecting everything to go perfectly can make the slightest hiccup seem much worse than it is. The common complications with phalloplasty are:

Infection

All surgeries come with a risk of infection, but there is more of a concern with phalloplasty as the wound sites are close to the anus. Infections are typically treated with antibiotics and tend to respond well.

Haematoma

A haematoma is when there is bleeding under the skin and the blood gathers and pools under the skin. It is like a large bruise. Haematomas do not usually need any surgical repair, but speak to your surgeon if you have a haematoma and it is painful or putting pressure or strain on your stitches.

Wound dehiscence

Dehiscence is when the two edges of an incision do not heal together. Wound healing issues can occur in around 11 per cent of phalloplasty surgeries but usually can be fixed.[3]

Partial or full phallic loss

Yes, it can happen. Full phallic loss, meaning the whole shaft of the penis would need to be removed, happens around 1.7 per cent of the time. A partial loss can happen around 7 per cent of the time.[4]

Complications if you have the urethra lengthened
Stricture

A stricture is when there is a full or partial blockage of the urethra. It can happen if the new urethra starts to heal itself together. The surgeon would then need to repair the urethra.

Fistula

A fistula is when a passage is created between two areas that don't normally connect. In the case of phalloplasty, it can happen between the new urethra and outside of the penis, creating a kind of second hole for peeing from. These can heal on their own over time, or sometimes they will need a repair once the rest of the penis has healed.

---

3   Heston, A.L., Esmonde, N.O. and Berli, J.U. (2019). Phalloplasty: Techniques and outcomes. *Translational Andrology and Urology, 8*(3), 254–265. https://doi.org/10.21037/tau.2019.05.05

4   Heston, A.L., Esmonde, N.O. and Berli, J.U. (2019). Phalloplasty: Techniques and outcomes. *Translational Andrology and Urology, 8*(3), 254–265. https://doi.org/10.21037/tau.2019.05.05

Urethra stricture and fistula rates are high, and they can occur in more than half of patients. Most instances, though, can be corrected.[5]

Retained vaginal mucosa

Sometimes when a vaginectomy is performed, there are some mucosal cells left behind and this can lead to a mucocele forming. Mucocele are benign cystic lesions. This would require a revision surgery.

Final thing

From the day you first decide to have phalloplasty to the final stage can be a long time. It's a marathon, so pace yourself. Don't think about it all the time. There can be long gaps where there is nothing to do but save money and wait to hear back about your next appointment. Find ways to put it out of your mind. Keep getting on with your life; don't put everything on hold until after you have a new penis.

JACK'S STORY

Jack is 34 and lives in Sussex. He had Stage 1 of phalloplasty using the forearm method seven years ago. Jack talked to me about the process of going through the surgery and recovery, and the difficulties he was having losing weight to have the next stage of surgery.

At the moment I'm halfway through. I had Stage 1 in 2014 – that was the phalloplasty using the arm, plus they put one testicle prosthesis in. And then during the recovery I put back on all the weight I'd lost for the surgery and I've been struggling with my weight ever since, so there's been a massive delay before Stage 2.

But the delay has actually given me time to think. I guess I

5   Louie, M. and Moulder, J.K. (2017). Hysterectomy for the transgender man. *Current Obstetrics and Gynecology Reports, 6,* 126–132. https://doi. org/10.1007/s13669-017-0211-5

thought to be a "correct" trans man I have to go through all the steps. But I've had time now to settle into who I actually am as a person and nail down what I want from my transition. I've realised I'm ace (asexual), and I don't want the erectile device anymore. It seems pointless putting myself through complicated surgery and recovery, maybe revisions, when I won't use it. I still need to lose weight, though, so the urethra extension will heal up and work properly, otherwise the weight puts too much pressure on the tube and it might end up narrowing.

First thinking about lower surgery

I've thought about lower surgery and then stopped thinking about it more than once. I vaguely worked out I was trans when I was about 15. Then I went into full-swing denial for six years and pointedly stopped thinking about lower surgery, and then it started creeping back in as I started transitioning.

I definitely looked at phalloplasty and metoidioplasty, because I wanted to make sure I had all the information. I knew you get better sensation with the meta, but the aesthetic side of it was more important; I wanted it to look as natural as possible and I had a better chance of that with phallo.

Being asexual and gender dysphoria

When I started the phalloplasty process I was very sex averse, and I assumed it was because I didn't have the right kit. I had less dysphoria about it being female genitalia, and more from the lack of male genitalia. I was always feeling inadequate, like I wasn't living up to my partner's expectations. But they were never the other person's expectations, they're what I *thought* the other person's expectations were. So they're *my* expectations.

I still probably would have chosen phallo if I'd worked out I was ace beforehand. When I get to the point where I can stand to pee, it will be even better. But just having the penis there is great.

Recovery

You can end up putting the day of the surgery on a pedestal, but you have to think about the recovery afterwards. Don't do it by yourself. I shouldn't have stayed in my flat alone. My mum was dropping in, and I had the district nurse coming round, but I did most of that recovery by myself and it was really hard. I needed someone there all of the time just in case.

I ended up putting on nearly two stone in weight in about six weeks because all I could do was lay down and eat chips. That was literally it. For the first three weeks I couldn't even watch TV, I was in too much pain, and I was too tired. Sat there in a flat by myself when I couldn't even turn the TV on was horrifically depressing. And the surgery is emotionally massive also. Trying to deal with that on my own at the same time as dealing with pain was not a good idea for my mental health.

It took a few weeks, but once I started to feel a bit more human I got excited that it was done, and I could look at it and get used to how it's part of me, and it's where it should be now. And I started to have a bit more self-acceptance.

At first people clocked the scar on my arm, but they don't now so much because I have the tattoo over it. Because of the shape it is, people are aware it's a skin graft and therefore I think a bit more cautious about the way they ask you what it's from. And if they do ask, 90 per cent of the time they don't ask what for. I just say it's a skin graft and they say, okay.

I think it was day three after surgery that it started feeling like part of me. They did a Doppler test on the penis to see if they could hear the pulse in it, and I think it was that moment. I'd spent the first couple of days groggy and there's so many bandages I couldn't tell what's penis and what's bandage. So when that was peeled away and I could move a bit, then I became aware of its existence, as its own little thing. Then all of a sudden I could hear my heartbeat through it and I realised, it's actually a part of me now. Once that clicked, I couldn't think about it not being there. My brain says, well yeah this is how it's supposed to be. I've been telling you this since day dot. It's odd. Your brain just accepts what your body is supposed to be doing.

10

Vaginoplasty, Vulvoplasty and Orchiectomy

This chapter covers the lower surgery options for trans and non-binary people who are born with a penis. "Lower surgery" is a general term for all of the genital surgeries for trans and non-binary people. For people born with a penis, there are three different options for lower surgery:

- **Orchiectomy.** Removing the testicles and scrotum, but keeping the penis.
- **Vulvoplasty and clitoroplasty.** Creating external genitalia but without a deep vagina. This means removing the penis and testicles and creating a vulva and clitoris, but without a vagina.
- **Vaginoplasty.** Removing the penis and testicles and creating a vulva, clitoris and vagina, plus shortening the urethra.

Here's a diagram of the anatomy we're going to be talking about, in case some of it isn't familiar to you. It's a generalised picture, because genitals come in a wide range of shapes and sizes. Take a look at thevulvagallery.com for a huge range of illustrations based on real vulvas to get a good idea of the variety. Also, www.thelabialibrary.org.au has a collection of photos to help demonstrate the range of ways a healthy vulva can look.

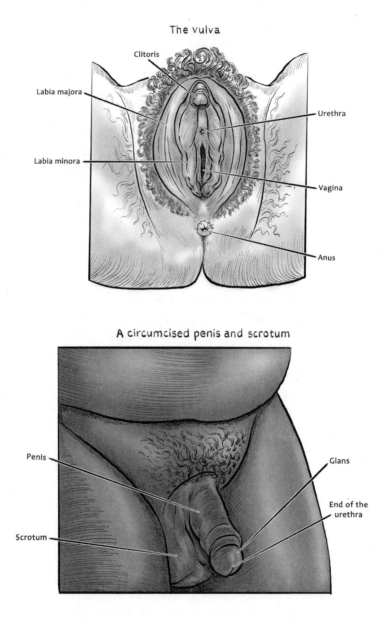

The vulva

Clitoris

Labia majora

Urethra

Labia minora

Vagina

Anus

A circumcised penis and scrotum

Penis

Glans

End of the
urethra

Scrotum

All three surgeries in this chapter are irreversible. If you have
an orchiectomy, you could later possibly have testicle implants
put into your scrotum, if you didn't have the skin of the scrotum
removed. If you have a vulvoplasty or vaginoplasty, tissue from

the penis and scrotum is all used to make the vagina, vulva and clitoris. It can't be turned back into a penis.

It is not possible currently to transplant a uterus into a body to enable a trans woman or non-binary person assigned male at birth to become pregnant and give birth. Transplanted uteruses from one person to another have been occurring since 2014, but only between people assigned female at birth. While it could be possible for a trans woman or non-binary person assigned male at birth to have a uterus transplanted, no one is offering this service, and it remains theoretical.

Orchiectomy

An orchiectomy is when the testicles are removed from inside the scrotum. The surgeon makes an incision in the scrotum and the testicles and spermatic cord are removed. The skin from the scrotum is usually used in the construction of a vagina and vulva. So the surgeon can perform the incision in such a way as to give you the option of a vaginoplasty later. But excess skin from the scrotum can also be removed if you are certain you will not want a vaginoplasty in the future.

Because the testicles produce testosterone, removing them reduces or removes the need for anti-androgens. If you take oes-trogen, you might also be able to lower the amount of oestrogen you take if you want to. Some doctors recommend speaking with your endocrinologist to adjust your hormones before sur-gery, so you can test how it feels to have a different balance. A sudden drop in testosterone can cause mood swings.

Orchiectomy is considered a low-risk surgery and can be done as an outpatient appointment, meaning you might not need to be kept overnight in hospital. Before surgery you will be invited to a consultation. The surgeon is likely to want to have a look at your testicles and check for anything that will interfere with the surgery, such as scarring or a hernia.

Some people choose orchiectomy as a first step towards hav-ing vaginoplasty, or as a surgery to have while they are deciding if they want a vulvoplasty or vaginoplasty. For others, orchiectomy is their preferred surgery, and they do not choose further genital surgery. Orchiectomy is also an option for people if they want to reduce their genital dysphoria but they are not eligible for vaginoplasty.

Of course not all trans and non-binary people have genital dysphoria, and some may just want to remove the need for taking anti-androgens.

After orchiectomy

People are expected to only need a few days to recover from an orchiectomy, but recovery is different for different people. As with all surgery, listen to your body, and take the time you need. Having erections and orgasms are both still possible after an orchiectomy, but you may find your sex drive has dropped or it is harder to have an erection or an orgasm. The advantages of an orchiectomy are it is a relatively low-risk surgery, and the recovery time is usually short. As with all surgeries, there is a risk of complications. Bleeding, infection and haematoma (a large painful bruise due to bleeding under skin) can occur.

> An assumption some people make is that if a trans woman chooses not to have a vaginoplasty, she must enjoy having a penis. I see nothing wrong with a trans woman liking her penis. But for me, that's not the case. It's just there. It's not a feature I've held on to as an asset. I simply didn't see the need to alter my body more than necessary.
>
> Inés

Vaginoplasty

This surgery creates a vagina, vulva and clitoris using the skin of the penis and scrotum. If needed, skin from other parts of the body, such as the urethra and colon, can also be used.

Different surgeons use slightly different techniques. There are pros and cons to each method, and the reason behind your surgeon feeling one is better for you than another should be based on your own anatomy.

Vaginoplasty and vulvaplasty

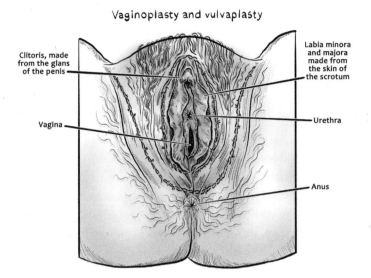

The system for making the vagina is similar in each surgery. A space is made between the back of the bladder and the rectum in preparation for the vagina being placed there. (A space needs to be made because the body doesn't typically leave spaces; all the organs sit close together.) The penis is disassembled into different parts. The urethra is separated from the rest of the penis ready to be repositioned under the new clitoris. The glans of the penis is trimmed down so it is smaller and shaped into a clitoris. The tissue containing nerves and blood vessels attached to the new clitoris is gently folded back so the clitoris can be placed in position. The clitoral hood is created from prepuce skin (foreskin) folded over the clitoris. The position of the clitoris is then a point of reference for the rest of the anatomy to be crafted around.

Next, the skin from the penis and scrotum is placed inside the space to create the vaginal canal, and it is packed with lubricated vaginal packing to prevent the new vagina from closing up. Labia majora are created from skin from the scrotum, and then the urethra is trimmed to the right length and positioned below the clitoris. It lies in the same position as it would on natal vulva, sometimes a little lower. Some surgeons sew the labia majora together for a few days to hold the vaginal packing in place.

Plus, a catheter (a tube in your urethra that drains pee into a bag) is kept in place until the vaginal packing is removed a few days later. This method of using the penis for most or all of the vagina is called penile inversion.

There may not be enough skin from the penis to make a vagina deep enough for penetrative sex. This can happen because the penis has shrunk from the impact of taking oestrogen or from taking hormone blockers during adolescence. Plus, some people's penises are smaller than others. This is when tissue from the scrotum, urethra or colon may also be used. After having a vaginoplasty, you have to dilate the new vagina so it doesn't close up. You need to do this regularly for the rest of your life. There is more information about this in the following sections.

Colovaginoplasty

Another technique for creating the vagina is to use a piece of the colon. The colon is part of the large intestine, the tubes in the stomach that remove nutrients and water from the food we eat. The colon connects to the small intestine at one end and becomes the rectum at the other.

Similar steps are followed for creating the vagina, but the penis is mostly removed apart from the glans, which can still be positioned as the clitoris. When the vagina is being created, a piece of colon is removed and the two ends of the colon sewn together.

The advantage of using colon tissue is it is naturally hairless and the skin creates its own mucus, so it is naturally self-lubricating.

The disadvantages are that it involves an additional step in the surgery, removing a piece of bowel. And with this step there is the risk of leaks in the bowel, which can lead to infection. The technique has become less popular because it can create too much mucus and leave the vagina with a bad smell.

Which method for creating the vagina is right for you is something to discuss with your surgeon when they look at your body.

The prostate is not removed as part of lower surgery for trans women and non-binary people, which means if you have this surgery you will still need to be aware of the signs and symptoms of prostate problems, including prostate cancer. Prostate problems are more likely to affect people over the age of 50. There is more about this in Chapter 16: Sexual Health and Check-Ups.

Vulvoplasty

A vulvoplasty creates a vulva, including the labia and clitoris, but it doesn't create any vaginal depth. The penis, testicles and scrotum are used to create the labia majora and minora and the clitoris in a very similar manner to vaginoplasty. It is sometimes called zero-depth vaginoplasty or limited-depth vaginoplasty.

The advantage of a vulvoplasty is the risks are lower, because most of the risks that come with vaginoplasty are related to the creation of the vagina itself. Also, you do not need to have hair removal in advance, and you won't need to dilate after the surgery, which is a lifelong commitment. You won't be able to have vaginal sex, but sexual sensation and being able to orgasm are still kept.

The disadvantage is it is not possible to later change your mind and decide to have a vaginoplasty. It is unlikely you will be able to have the vagina added later because the tissues from the genitals used to build and line the vagina will no longer be available.

There are still risks with vulvoplasty, of course, as there are with all surgery. Bleeding, infection and numbness around the vulva can occur. Your surgeon should discuss all the risks before you agree to have surgery.

Some hospitals require you to stop smoking before they will perform a vaginoplasty. This could mean stopping smoking for several weeks prior to surgery and continuing not to smoke afterwards. See Chapter 12: Preparing for Surgery for information on why surgeons ask people to stop smoking and some advice on how to stop.

An alternative to lower surgery: Tucking

Tucking is pulling your genitals back between your legs and holding them in place to create a flatter appearance. The penis can be tucked between the legs or between the buttocks, and the testicles can be gently pushed back up into the inguinal canals: the spaces where they descended from.

Tucking can be done safely and shouldn't be painful, though it can be uncomfortable. If you haven't done it before, take your time. Gently poke the testicles up into the inguinal canal and then pull the penis back and hold it in place with medical tape or tight underwear. Some people also wear a gaff – a piece of clothing worn over underwear when tucking to ensure everything stays in place. You can make your own or buy them online. You can also just use a second pair of underwear or a feminine pad or thin sanitary towel.

When you untuck, take the same care to move your body back. Be sure to keep everything clean and dry, especially in hot weather, to avoid damage to your skin.

Tucking tips:

- If you use tape, only use medical tape. Don't use duct tape; it can damage your skin. You can find medical tape in a pharmacy. You can also find "tucking tape" in online stores.
- Shave the area you are putting tape on so you don't pull all the hair out later when you remove the tape.
- Plan ahead – tucking with tape is more secure than not, but it will make it more difficult to go to the bathroom, and it will mean you need to carry extra tape with you.
- Take care of your skin. Tucking with tape every day can irritate or rip your skin, especially in hot weather.
- Don't tuck so tightly you cut off blood supply to the penis.

Going for a consultation

If you are thinking about lower surgery but still have questions and aren't even sure if it is right for you, it can still be helpful to go to a consultation and speak to a surgeon. This is an opportunity to ask for the latest information about different surgical techniques and options and find out what is going to work for your individual body, as well as how your health and medical needs might impact your recovery.

Not all surgical services offer orchiectomy, vulvoplasty and vaginoplasty. And some services may only offer one method for vaginoplasty. It's important to know what your options are and where you can go to find the service right for you.

Here is a list of suggested questions for the surgeon:

- How do you perform the vaginoplasty?
- What technique is right for me?
- What are the risks?
- Do I need to stop smoking?
- Do I need to remove hair, and if so where from?
- When can I have the surgery? Can I pick a time that suits me a bit better?
- Do I need to do any preparation?
- How long will I be in hospital?
- What are the common complications? How are they resolved?
- What will it be like when I wake up? Will I be able to sit or just lie down?
- How long will I be off work? (And let them know if you have a physically demanding job.)
- How long until I can start swimming/running/cycling?
- How long until I can have sex or masturbate?
- If I have complications when I'm home, who do I contact?
- I will need a sick note for work or studying. Where do I get this from?
- Do you provide dilators?
- How much is the surgery and what does that cost cover? Does it cover fixing any complications? (If you will be paying for surgery yourself.)

Preparing for surgery

There are a few things you can do to prepare for surgery. Your surgeon may ask you to stop taking oestrogen prior to surgery, or to switch to a lower dose. This lowers the risk of deep vein thrombosis. There are also things to buy in advance, so you have them in your house when you come home from hospital:

- water-based lubrication for dilation. Get a lot. You'll be doing it three times a day
- old towels for lying on when you're douching and dilating
- dilators if the hospital isn't providing them
- antibiotic ointment for cleaning the suture sites
- sanitary towels or feminine pads (the kind people wear when they have a period)
- loose underpants that you don't mind throwing away. They can get stained with blood as you heal. Get them baggy as you don't want pressure on your new vagina
- a handheld mirror to hold between your legs so you can see your new anatomy. Try to get one with a handle so you can easily see at different angles.

Hair removal for vaginoplasty

If you choose to have a vaginoplasty, you will need to have all the hair removed from the penis and probably the scrotum. This is because tissues from both of these organs can be used to create the vaginal canal, and it is essential that this skin is hairless with no chance of hair growing back. If you do not have hair removal before surgery there is the risk of hair balls, blockages and chronic infections in your vagina. At your consultation, your surgeon can advise on which areas of the penis and scrotum need to be hairless.

Electrolysis is always a permanent form of hair removal because it destroys the hair root. A thin wire is inserted into each hair follicle and then an electric current is passed down the wire to destroy the root. It will feel hot or stinging when the current passes.

Laser hair removal is also offered sometimes as a permanent hair removal technique, but the results can be more varied. The contrast between your skin tone and hair colour can affect how well laser hair removal works. Laser can work well on pale skin with dark hair, but it is less successful on darker skin with lighter hair. Laser hair removal does not guarantee a permanent hair removal, which is essential for vaginoplasty.

Hair removal can be time consuming and expensive, because each hair needs to be destroyed individually. You can spread the cost by having less frequent visits to the electrolysist, but this will mean the whole process will take longer.

Hair removal on your genitals can be awkward and trigger gender dysphoria. It is a difficult procedure to go through for many trans and non-binary people. Try asking local trans and non-binary people in your area who they went to see to get a good recommendation.

Being in hospital

An orchiectomy may mean an overnight stay in hospital, but a vulvoplasty or vaginoplasty is more likely to mean a few days in hospital.

When you wake up, you will have a lot of bandages and padding around your new vagina, plus a catheter, so you won't need to get up to pee. You may have drains coming out of your body and packing in your vagina. Different surgeons use slightly different methods, so be sure to ask about what has been placed and when things will be removed if you're not sure.

You will be discharged when the surgeon is happy with your healing. They will need to know you have successfully peed after the catheter was removed, a sign there is no damage to your urethra.

Complications

Like with all surgery, sometimes there are complications. Often a minor problem will correct itself; other times you will need a revision surgery. It can be stressful when everything doesn't go according to plan, so it's good to be aware ahead of time of the common complications. As well as bleeding and infection, the common complications after vaginoplasty are:

Stenosis
This is when the vagina loses depth. It can occur if you don't dilate enough. Any depth lost can't be recovered.

Fistula
A fistula is when a passage is created between two areas inside the body that don't normally connect. In vaginoplasty, it can happen between the new urethra and vagina, or between the rectum and the vagina.

Prolapse
This means all or part of the vagina protrudes out of the body. It can happen when a haematoma forms in the vagina.

Dehiscence
Dehiscence is when a wound starts to reopen. It is a common complication with vaginoplasty, but it can be managed without surgical intervention.

It is not a common complication, but vaginoplasty can result in a reduced orgasm, or loss of orgasm. Speak to your surgeon about the chances of this happening if you are concerned.

Dilating
If you have vaginoplasty, dilation is an essential, lifelong part of keeping a vagina. Dilating involves regularly inserting a smooth, tube-shaped device into your vagina to prevent it starting to close up. It is important in the same way that wearing earrings is important for keeping the pierced holes in your ears. If you don't keep up a regular routine of dilating (or having penetrative sex

with a dildo or penis), then you will start to lose vaginal depth, and it cannot be regained.

Dilating can be difficult and time consuming at first. But it gets easier, and as time goes on it doesn't have to be done as frequently. Typically it starts with fifteen minutes, three times a day, but it eventually drops down to once every other day. Because it is so important, it is key to factor in the private time and space you'll need to lie down and dilate when planning time off work or study.

You will probably start dilating while you're still in hospital, where the nurses can show you the technique and guide you through it. Some hospitals will give you a kit of dilators to take home, though others require you to buy them yourself. Dilators come in a range of girths, with markers along the shaft so you can keep track of how deep it has gone. You start with the thinnest dilator, using lots of water-based lube, and move up gradually to a thicker one.

Once you're home, there are videos from medical professionals and trans women and non-binary people discussing dilating tips and good practice on YouTube.

Tips for dilating:

- Lie down, get comfy and give yourself some time to relax before starting.
- Use a pillow under your bum to help find a good angle.
- Use a small mirror to help you see your vagina and find where to angle the dilator.
- Use an old towel underneath your bum as you dilate, as lube and a little blood can come out. It can sometimes get messy.

Douching

Once you have healed, your new vagina will need to be cared for. Natal vaginas keep themselves clean and do not need to be washed inside, but a vagina created by vaginoplasty does not have the mix of mucus and good bacteria a natal vagina does.

In the early days after surgery, when you are dilating three times a day, it can be a good idea to douche inside your vagina to keep it clean. Unscented antibacterial soap and warm water works fine; you do not need to buy expensive products. To clean inside your vagina you will need a douche, a device similar to a turkey baster, that can squirt warm soapy liquid inside. You can buy these cheaply from an online chemist. If you have any smelly or unusual discharge, speak to a doctor.

Having sex with your vagina for the first time

Your new vagina or vulva will take some time to heal. It could be tempting to masturbate out of curiosity, boredom or frustration. But in general, you want to treat your new vagina or vulva and the areas around it very gently at first. It is best to not have sex until you are fully healed. This can take at least three months, sometimes longer. Before having penetrative sex for the first time, some people find it useful to dilate to prevent feeling too tight.

Most people report being able to orgasm after lower surgery. Studies suggest many people experience a different quality of orgasm, though, and talk about a "new" type of orgasm that is more intense, smoother and longer.

Final thing

Lower surgery can be a big physical journey to go through, but it can also be a big emotional journey. It can be a lot to deal with all at once – having new genitals, healing and dealing with the stress of any complications. Having supportive people around you, in person or online, can be helpful as you get to know your new body.

MIKEY'S STORY

Mikey is 21 years old and lives in Maryland, USA. I spoke to Mikey ten months after her vaginoplasty.

So I came out in 2016 and straight after that I started thinking about surgery. That's what I wanted and that's how I was going to become who I am.

I've always felt very weird having a penis. I wasn't as bad as many people are; I could still be sexually active. I didn't like it, but it wasn't debilitating. It was more that I didn't have the female body I would be comfortable in. Then as I started transitioning, I started becoming more dysphoric. It's a pain in the butt, when you have a penis and you're living as a woman.

When I came out to my parents at 16, they told me I was paying for everything. I did not know how I was going to do it, but I turned 18 and started transitioning, without them knowing. I've probably spent about ten thousand dollars of my own money throughout my entire transition.

One big thing I would say to anyone considering surgery is research the heck out of any surgeon you are considering. What really helped me was seeing a video on YouTube – literally a cartoon simulation of the surgery. That helped me understand what was going to happen, and made me more comfortable, and familiar with the process of the surgery I was going to have.

I booked a consultation, but it was going to take two and a half years. Then I found another surgeon, who is also a trans woman, that took four or five months. But she didn't take insurance. Then my therapist told me about a surgeon who is just twenty minutes from my house. I looked into it and phenomenal things were said about him, so I decided I was going to go with him: he's close, he takes insurance and everything worked out perfectly.

To get a consultation I had to get my two referral letters.[1] Once I had the consultation, the surgeon wanted me to have a pelvic MRI so he knew where to place the canal and the parts of the vagina before going in. I also had to have an

---

1   Before 2022 you needed two referral letters for vaginoplasty, but the WPATH Standards of Care now only recommend one letter.

appointment with a pelvic floor physical therapist to learn how to work the new configuration of my muscles.

Another thing I did was hair removal. Laser hair removal hurts. The more treatments you have the easier it gets, because it hurts most when it's the most thick. Having the hair removal was really weird. I think the weirdest part is when she had to touch it. She was an older lady and she tried to make conversation during it which was great; she was sweet, but it was awkward.

On the day of the surgery, it was scary. I think I was in so much shock that it was about to happen, I remember being numb to the entire day before. But I was so unbelievably excited.

Everybody said, oh my god when you wake up, you're going to feel totally different; it's going to feel like there's no testosterone. But I didn't really feel that in the moment. I think I just felt relaxed for the first time in my life. It also could have been the drugs! I just felt whole.

When I had surgery, the skin graft, which was the lining of my vagina, didn't adhere to the walls as it was supposed to do, which is okay; it happens. So it was removed and instead of a skin graft from scrotal tissue it was then just lined with the scar tissue that forms over time. But as the scar tissue formed, it tightened the canal, making it harder for it to stretch, harder to dilate. It was taking me three and half hours to dilate every day. So I had revisions to the vaginoplasty when I had breast augmentation; they opened it back up and now it's all good to go. Dilator goes right in, thirty minutes and we're good.

The first week after coming home from the hospital, you're sitting in a room all day, every day, you don't move, and you can get very depressed. It's just post-op depression. I called it my post-vagina depression. It's very natural to feel that with any surgery. You're healing, your body's using so much energy. You're just not in a good state mentally. It was really hard, and I was so depressed and at some points having inactive feelings of suicide. I wouldn't have acted on those feelings, but I felt awful.

So we had a tough go at the beginning. But as it healed, and as I healed, I fell in love with my vagina, and I fell in love with who I became. It's now a very special part of me that I would not give up.

INÉS'S STORY

Inés is 49 and lives in South London. She talked to me about choosing to have an orchiectomy in 2017.

I was not one of those people who had their gender figured out at three or four. It was more like a puzzle I pieced together while growing up. Through my late teens, I tried to settle on a queer identity I was comfortable with. I was often flamboyantly genderqueer – although, back then, I didn't have that vocabulary and knew very little about other trans people. It all hit home at 19 when I realised that, more than anything, I yearned to be female. But I was deeply isolated, and my identity felt like a recipe for social rejection – even among queer cis friends – so I backed away from transitioning.

Through my 20s and 30s, I was dimly conscious of the slow blossoming of trans visibility. Each year, at queer film festivals, I would seek out films that featured trans people. And I would sit in the cinema thinking, this is what I should be doing...if I were only brave enough!

Eventually, I just hit a turning point where I let go of my old fears. I didn't know how life as a woman would work out, but at least I would be moving on from that mute frustration I had felt for two decades. So I socially transitioned in 2013. About halfway through that year, I started on HRT: oestrogen at first, and then six months later, I began injections to suppress testosterone.

I was probably 15 when I had my first vague thoughts about gender confirmation surgery, and I was 45 when I had my operation, so the thought had been developing for quite some time! My initial plans for my transition involved a vaginoplasty. But as I did more research, I began to question if a vagina was truly necessary to my life. In the accounts I had read by other trans women, the impact of a vaginoplasty was always psychologically profound, but frequently physically traumatic. And I lacked the necessary determination to put my body through that. I wanted some form of genital surgery but didn't view having a vagina as an essential end goal of my transition.

When I was first offered an appointment to discuss surgery at the gender clinic, I actually asked to delay it for a year, as I wasn't confident I had made up my mind at that point. I wanted to experience how my body was changing on hormone replacement therapy (HRT), because that was already starting to affect the way I felt about genital surgery.

Choosing an orchiectomy

The information I was seeing about gender confirming surgery for trans women usually presented vaginoplasty as the only real option. Yet by this stage, I was more interested in orchiectomy.

I was clear I wanted my testes removed. The triptorelin injections I was having every twelve weeks are effectively a temporary medical castration and, after a few years of experiencing the results, I felt ready for the permanent solution. My body had feminised considerably, thanks to HRT. And my genitals had changed along with the rest of me. My penis no longer seemed so incongruously male. Now that I could view it as an appropriate part of my trans body, the idea of a major genital reconfiguration, such as vulvoplasty, became less compelling.

My guiding concern was long-term health and comfort, with sexual function only a minor consideration. Ever since my first injection, my libido has been almost indetectable. That doesn't bother me, but it has underlined how fragile sexual function can be. I was wary of elaborate reconstructive surgery, which I felt would entail added risks. So I settled on orchiectomy as the right choice for me.

When I talked my decision over with doctors, I met with

some pushback for not following the expected path. One psychiatrist at the gender clinic told me I would look "more convincingly female" if I opted for a vulvoplasty. Yet only my partner sees me naked. In everyday encounters, there are plenty of more conspicuous clues that affect how we read a person's gender or sex.

The gender clinic did end up approving my surgery referral, thankfully. But my surgical consultation felt like round two, with the urologist spending more time questioning my decision than explaining what the operation would involve. He kicked off by telling me an orchiectomy was a very unusual request, then speculated about how my penis could deter would-be sexual partners, leaving me frustrated and unloved. And I was warned, sternly, that my orchiectomy would not preserve sufficient tissue for a successful vaginoplasty, should I ever change my mind – an outcome the surgeon appeared to regard as all too probable. All this unsolicited counselling was patronising and, frankly, a little weird. Why was a doctor urging me to consider radical surgery that I wasn't asking for, on purely cosmetic grounds?

As the date got closer, I was fairly anxious. I had not faced significant surgery before and, in the week before my operation, a protective reflex had me questioning the wisdom of removing organs that were healthy, albeit unwanted. But I never came close to backing out. I guess I just needed to register that I was saying goodbye to parts of my body.

Healing from the orchiectomy took time. I expected to feel pain near the external wound and was surprised by a nagging ache deeper within my pelvis. I regretted not asking the surgeon for a diagram. Even now, I don't really know what happened to my insides in that operation.

After five days, it became time to steel myself, remove the dressing and take my first look. I remember lying flat on my bed once I finished washing, feeling almost euphoric with relief: Ahhh, I did it! By three weeks, I was feeling far less sore, though still delicate and easily tired. Within a month, however, I was strong enough to go to a friend's party and dance – cautiously, but joyfully. It felt like coming out the other side: a sign of being back to my usual self.

In one respect, the outcome of my surgery sometimes still disappoints me. My genitals limit what type of clothes I feel comfortable wearing, as I always feel mindful of my little bump. I had hoped my surgery would make this far less of an issue, since a good portion of my external genitalia was taken away. But I still have a challenge to find jeans that look good from the front, and alas, I'm not one for wearing skirts. So the orchiectomy hasn't really expanded my fashion choices in the way that a vulvoplasty might have done. That's a trade-off I live with.

I have come to like the way I don't look entirely female. My post-transition body has an interesting double-layered quality, a blend of male and female traits, thanks to the effects of testosterone and oestrogen at different stages of its history. I sometimes think of it as a "non-binary" body, and that's something I appreciate about it...on most days! And I feel that my genitals now are in harmony with that body. They are no longer conventionally male, by any stretch. But their remodelling has been relatively gentle, and they certainly look nothing like a conventional female body. It feels like the right outcome for me, one very much in line with my belief that all bodies are valid.

11

Vocal Surgery

Our voices and how we speak

The pitch of your voice is controlled by bands of soft tissue inside your larynx (voice box). These bands of tissue are your vocal folds. They're often called vocal cords. They are not really shaped like cords, more like tight curtains that can open, close and vibrate across the larynx. Our glottis is the opening between the vocal folds. As we speak, we expel air from our lungs. The air travels over the vocal folds, which vibrate to create the sound waves of our voice.

Vocal folds inside the larynx

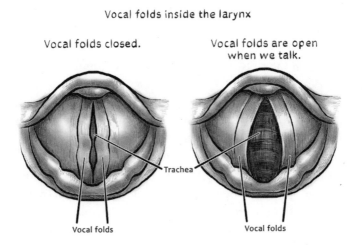

Vocal folds closed.

Vocal folds are open when we talk.

Trachea

Vocal folds

Vocal folds

The sound of our voice is made up of three parts:

- the basic sound we produce
- the resonance: how our throat, mouth cavity and nose passages modify and amplify the sound. This gives each person their unique voice
- the articulation: how the lips, tongue and soft palate turn sound into recognisable words.

There is more to how we speak than just the sound of our voice, though. There is breathiness, pitch, intensity and volume. Plus, we speak with more than just our voice; we speak with hand gestures, eye contact, different paces of speech and different rhythms. All these aspects can be used to give information about our gender.

During a male adolescence, the increase in testosterone in the body triggers physical changes, including the larynx growing larger and the vocal folds becoming thicker and longer.

Our vocal folds vibrate in a sequence of cycles at different typical speeds, producing different pitches that are heard as male, female or from a child:

110 cycles per second (men) = lower pitch
180 to 220 cycles per second (women) = medium pitch
300 cycles per second (children) = higher pitch.

But the length and thickness of our vocal folds also affect the pitch of our voice. Longer, thicker folds vibrate more slowly and produce lower notes, whereas thinner, shorter folds can produce higher notes. It is similar, in some ways, to the strings on a guitar or in a piano. One study looked at data on vocal folds and found, on average, the length of vocal folds in men was about 25 per cent longer than that of women.[1]

Other things can also affect the pitch of your voice, such as

---

1   Kim, H.T. (2020). Vocal feminization for transgender women: Current strategies and patient perspectives. *International Journal of General Medicine, 12*(13), 43–52. https://doi.org/10.2147/IJGM.S205102

smoking, having had vocal fold polyps or scarring from voice abuse.

Oestrogen therapy, for people transitioning to female, does not change the voice. Testosterone therapy for people transitioning to male in almost all cases deepens the voice into the male range.

If you are looking to change the way you speak so it better matches your gender, you have options for voice therapy and vocal surgery. Voice therapy aims to teach you how to use your body to raise or lower the pitch of your voice, plus adjust all the other aspects of how you speak to match your gender.

Perception of someone's pitch depends mostly on the fundamental frequency in the speaker's voice. This is the lowest note they can reach. The fundamental frequency of cisgender men is on average about an octave lower than cisgender women. Voice feminisation surgery focuses just on raising the fundamental frequency of your voice. This is done by making changes to the vocal folds to raise the lowest note you can reach. For voice masculinisation, the vocal folds are relaxed so deeper notes can be produced.

Voice feminisation therapy

Vocal feminisation therapy is highly recommended before using any surgical options, as well as in conjunction with surgery. Voice therapy works on all aspects of your voice and how you speak. Pitch is an important aspect of a voice being heard as female, but pitch alone is not always enough. Resonance and breathiness have been found to be important alongside pitch to create a voice recognised as female.

Some people can achieve the voice they want just through voice therapy. Also, voice therapy is a non-invasive process, whereas surgery is irreversible and always comes with risks. So it's advised to always start with voice therapy and see how much you can get out of it. If you choose to have surgery, continue having voice therapy afterwards to help you use your new voice.

Voice therapy will help you work on your:

- pitch (how high or low your voice sounds)
- resonance (the quality of the sound of your voice)
- intonation (the rhythm of your speech)
- rate (how fast or slow you speak)
- volume (how loud you speak).

Voice feminisation surgery

There are a few different forms of voice feminisation surgery. Voice feminisation surgery works in one of three ways: decreasing the length of the vocal folds, decreasing the density of the vocal folds or increasing the tension of the vocal folds. Both transgender and cisgender people have this surgery when wanting to raise their speaking voice.

Another surgery many trans and non-binary people have is an Adam's apple reduction. This is also known as a thyroid shave or reduction laryngoplasty. This reduces the size of the Adam's apple, but it does not affect the tone or pitch of your voice; it is just an aesthetic change. It is also known as a thyroid shave. There is more information on a reduction laryngoplasty in Chapter 6: Facial Feminisation Surgery.

What happens during surgery

Voice feminisation surgery happens under general anaesthetic. Your surgeon may use a laryngoscope to access your voice box. This is a thin, lighted tube that goes into your mouth and reaches back to your larynx. But some procedures require incisions on the outside of your throat.

Anterior glottic web formation or Wendler glottoplasty

This surgery raises the pitch of the voice by shortening the length of your vocal cords. This is the most common type of voice feminisation surgery. The vocal folds are shortened by creating a scar (or web) at the front of the vocal folds. This surgery also narrows the airway to some degree. As a result, it might be less appropriate for vocal professionals or serious athletes.

Cricothyroid approximation (CTA)

This surgery creates a higher pitch by increasing the tension in the vocal folds. CTA is also performed under general anaesthetic, but via an incision in the neck. Stitches are made in the cartilage of the voice box, decreasing the cricothyroid distance, which increases the tension in the vocal folds. However, studies have found that this method doesn't always have a lasting effect.[2]

There are disadvantages to this surgery. CTA is not suitable for people under 30. This is because the thyroid cartilage of younger patients has not formed a solid enough framework to prevent postoperative deformity.

Another problem with CTA is it can damage the cricothyroid (CT) muscle. The CT muscle is the most important muscle in the control of voice register. Damage to this muscle can reduce pitch range and create an unnatural falsetto sound.

Laser reduction glottoplasty (LRG)

A laser is used to remove the outer layers of the vocal folds. This decreases the mass, or density, of the vocal folds. This surgery is performed under general anaesthetic, using a thin tube passed down the throat.

Complications

Risks of bleeding or infection are low for these surgeries. Complications that can occur with voice surgery are around the surgery not producing an even, smooth voice. Surgery can leave

---

2 · Kim, H.T. (2020). Vocal feminization for transgender women: Current strategies and patient perspectives. *International Journal of General Medicine, 12*(13), 43–52. https://doi.org/10.2147/IJGM.S205102

your voice too high or so rough, hoarse, strained or breathy as to make talking difficult. When the surgery is performed down your throat, there is a small risk of damage to your teeth.

It is important to note that because voice feminisation surgery removes the ability to produce lower sounds, one consequence is you will lose the overall range of your voice.

Going for a consultation

Before you agree to surgery, go for a consultation with a surgeon to discuss your aims and be sure you fully understand the risks. At the consultation the surgeon may ask to record the sound of your voice and examine or take a video of your vocal folds as you make different types of sounds.

It is important, as always, to have realistic expectations of what voice feminisation surgery can achieve and what some of the outcomes might be. At your consultation, ask to hear examples of before and after results.

A consultation is an opportunity to ask lots of questions about the procedure, the different options and the experience of the surgeon. Here is a list of suggested questions:

- How does the surgery work?
- How much change in my voice can I expect?
- What are the risks to my voice, and how often do they happen?
- Will I lose the character of my own voice?
- How will it affect how I sing?
- How long does it take to recover?
- Will I be able to talk or whisper at all after the surgery?
- When do I know it's okay to start speaking?
- Will my throat be sore after surgery? What can I eat?
- If something seems wrong, who do I call?
- How long have you been performing this surgery?
- What percentage of your patients have a successful outcome? How many have no change?

- How much does the whole procedure cost and what does that cover?

Preparing for surgery

In preparation for surgery, your voice therapist may suggest exercises you can do before surgery to ensure your vocal folds are as healthy as possible.

When you look for a voice therapist, check their credentials and training. You may be looking for someone called a speech-language pathologist or speech therapist. Check to see if they have had specialised training on assessment and communication skills for trans people.

It is always worth speaking with former patients of the surgeons you are looking at to see what sorts of long-term changes they have had.

You may be asked to stop smoking for a few weeks before the surgery and not to smoke afterwards.

Recovery after surgery

Voice feminisation is sometimes done as an outpatient procedure, meaning you won't need to stay overnight in hospital. Other times you will be kept in for one night so they can observe how you are recovering.

You will not be able to talk after the surgery and will need to completely rest your voice for two weeks. You will need to avoid laughing, singing and coughing also. Have a range of ways to communicate non-verbally, such as on notes and text messages. If you have the surgery as an outpatient, you will need somebody to be with you when you go home and to stay with you for twenty-four hours. Drink lots of water to stay hydrated, and to reduce the need to cough.

After surgery, your voice will not have changed instantly. Sometimes people find their voice is deeper after surgery, but this can be caused by the swelling around the vocal folds and larynx. It generally takes around six weeks before you are able to find your new speaking range, and six months for any roughness to go away.

You are usually looking at around one to two weeks off work or study, and around a month before you should go back to exercise.

Your surgeon can advise on when your voice is ready to begin therapy again. This is usually around three weeks after surgery. Post-surgical voice therapy can help with resonance changes through exercises to relax the tongue and lips, improve resonance in the throat and for vowel modification.

Before surgery, the voice will have a low fundamental frequency and resonance frequency. After the surgery, the fundamental frequency rises but the resonance remains the same, thus creating a mismatch. Post-surgical voice therapy can help prevent you returning to your original resonance frequency.

Voice masculinisation surgery

If you choose to take testosterone, this is likely to lower your voice. Testosterone causes the vocal cords to get thicker and longer, and most people are happy with the new deepness.

Just as with voice feminisation, people are strongly advised to have a course of voice therapy before considering surgery. A voice therapist can help you use your voice in different ways and give you exercises to change the depth of your voice without straining.

However, if testosterone has not produced the effects you want, voice masculinisation surgery can relax the vocal folds to allow you to speak in a deeper voice. Just as shorter, tighter vocal cords can produce a higher pitch, longer, slacker vocal folds can produce lower tones.

Voice masculinising surgery is an outpatient procedure, and it is performed under local anaesthetic. This means you will be awake through the surgery, but you won't feel any pain in your throat. The surgery cannot be reversed.

The surgery to deepen the voice is called a type 3 thyroplasty. A 2–3 cm long incision is made in the front of the neck to reach the larynx. A small island of cartilage is cut away and pushed back, which allows the vocal folds to relax. As the surgeon adjusts the cartilage, the patient is able to speak and hear the changes in their voice. When they are happy with the changes, the surgeon will stop.

Patients can hear the change in their voices immediately and can start using the new voice straight away; there isn't a need to rest the voice. However, working with a voice therapist after surgery is still recommended, and it can take a few months for the voice to adjust and for each patient to feel comfortable speaking in the new range.

Final thing

Using a new voice takes time and lots of practice. Just like with a lot of the surgeries in this book, it is a good idea to have some friends around you, in person or online, who are going through the same things as you. They can share tips and ideas, plus offer support if you are frustrated with your progress.

12

Preparing for Surgery

Whatever surgery you have coming up, there are things you can do in advance to try to make the whole process run as smoothly as possible.

Get referred for surgery

The WPATH Standards of Care recommend you have one referral from a professional trained in gender identity.

The referral is just a letter, printed or emailed, from a professional with experience assessing transgender people. It will detail what surgery you would like and how you meet the criteria set out in the standards of care.

This letter or email is then sent to the surgical service. The surgical service will then get in touch with you, directly or via your GP or mental health professional, and arrange a consultation.

If you are already in touch with a transgender clinic, they will be able to advise you on arranging the referral. There is not a transgender service in every city; you may need to travel to another city to use a service there.

If you are using or have used a mental health service where you talked about your trans or non-binary identity, they may be able to provide one of the letters of referral.

If you have just realised you are trans or non-binary, or you have known for a long time but never told anyone, you will probably need to get a formal diagnosis of gender dysphoria from a mental health professional before you can access either hormone therapy or gender confirmation surgery. Frustrating as this can be, it does at least give you time to be fully informed about the options available to you.

Arrange support

Try to arrange to have people around you to support you with the whole surgical journey. There are bound to be all kinds of things you may need help or support with, or times when you would just like a friend with you. For example:

- going to the consultation
- talking through your options
- keeping you company going into hospital
- looking after your pets
- visiting you and bringing you things in hospital
- helping you get home, driving you or carrying bags
- helping you at home with medical care or shopping
- help with washing or showering is sometimes needed
- generally chatting and helping you deal with stress.

Work and education

Some gender confirmation surgeries require several weeks of recovery. If you work or are in education, you will need to let them know you are taking time off. Be realistic about how much time you need. You do not need to tell your work what surgery you are having if you don't want to. As you are preparing for surgery, be sure to familiarise yourself with your employer's sick leave policy – how much time you can take off, how much notice you need to give and anything else you should know in advance.

If you are able to pick when your surgery is scheduled, consider using education holidays or when there is a less busy time at work. There may be other factors to consider when picking the right time:

- When you can best take time off work or education with the least amount of stress.
- When you can get help from a friend or someone in your family during recovery. You may need someone to drive you home from the hospital, or come home with you on the train or bus and help carry your bags.
- When you can recover at home easily. This might mean factoring in school holidays if you have children.
- If you are in work, how much sick leave you have and when you can take it.
- If you are self-employed, when is convenient for you to take time off and what impact that will have on your income.

Things to have with you in hospital

Managing a stay in hospital is a key part of recovery from surgery. It is easy to become bored, stressed, anxious and depressed. So plan in advance how to spend your time.

You will be spending a lot of time in bed, mostly lying down, or just raised up a bit. You may be in some pain at times, or uncomfortable, so gentle and engrossing activities, plus a range of activities so you can keep switching between them, can be good. You know yourself and how you deal with being cooped up.

Things that can help kill time to take with you:

- headphones, music and podcasts downloaded onto your phone or mp3 player; films or TV shows downloaded onto your phone; audiobooks
- extra data on your phone in case there isn't Wi-Fi so you can message friends and family
- games and puzzles you can play on your phone or tablet. Lots of games are available for free
- small, light books or comics (it will be difficult to sit up and read heavier ones), or an eBook reader (an easy way to carry a huge selection of books!). Also see if your local library runs an eBook service. Many libraries do this, and

you can borrow, read and return books and audiobooks for free on your phone or tablet using an app
- magazines, or a magazine subscription on a tablet
- crafts that you like, doodling, crochet, colouring, word games.

Other useful things to have with you:

- wet wipes or face wipes to help you wash without having to move too much. Also a toothbrush, soap and a small hand towel
- sugar-free gum to chew after meals to give your teeth a clean if you find it hard to get out of bed
- loose clothes that you don't need to put over your head. If you are having surgery on your chest, it might be sore to raise your arms
- underwear and loose pyjamas
- slippers with non-slip soles. You might find it hard to reach your feet at first for putting socks on
- a small amount of money
- snacks in case you get hungry. Food is served at fixed times in hospitals, and you may get choices each day often including vegetarian, vegan and gluten-free options. But it's useful to have extra food to make sure you don't get hungry, especially if you don't like the food served or have a restricted diet
- things to help you sleep. Everyone sleeps in different positions and moves around in the night. You are likely to find, though, that you can only sleep on your back after surgery. If you are not used to sleeping on your back, this can make it hard to sleep. Try practising before you go into hospital. You may also find a neck support pillow helpful.

Bring with you information that the hospital staff may ask for: a list of any medication you're on and how much you take; your GP's name, address and phone number; information about other important people who help care for you; a list of anything you are allergic to; and the names of any previous operations you have had, including ones as a child.

Prepare your home for recovery

It can be a good idea to prepare your home for when you come out of hospital. You might be uncomfortable sitting down on a chair so you spend more time in bed or lying on the sofa. Depending on how your home is set up, you therefore might want things around you in easy reach of the bed or sofa, wherever you'll spend most time resting. Make sure you have things like your books or magazines, laptop or TV easily accessible.

You will probably be more tired than usual when you come out of hospital, and you might find you have less concentration for the things you usually spend time on.

Have the fridge and freezer a bit stocked for a few days' worth of food that is easy to prepare.

Things to stock up on:

- tins
- staples like bread, pasta, cereal, milk, tea or coffee, vegetables or whatever you eat regularly
- pet food
- ready meals.

When you leave hospital, you will probably be given a bag of all the medicines and bandages you need. But it's a good idea to stock your bathroom up with other supplies you may need:

- soap
- face wash
- painkillers
- gauze
- medical tape
- bandages
- safety pins.

It is common to find it difficult to do a poo after you have had surgery. One common side effect of the painkiller codeine is constipation. So get some laxatives in to help move your bowels if you have this problem; it can be very uncomfortable.

Also, if you are having genital surgery, the incisions can be very near to your anus. Of course, you want to keep your wounds clean and free from infection while also not getting them wet. Try using moist toilet paper or wet wipes to clean your bum after you go to the toilet. They can be easier to use when you are trying to avoid touching your incisions too much while they heal.

Consultation

There can be a lot of information to take in at a consultation. And it is easy to feel under pressure when you have been looking forward to surgery or saving up a long time. Whenever you go for a consultation, there are some ways you can help yourself get the most out of it:

- Start noting down questions you want to ask in the days or weeks leading up to the consultation.
- Take the list of your questions with you.
- Take someone with you; they can take notes while you listen.
- Record the consultation on your phone (let the surgeon know).
- Ask the surgeon to repeat anything that wasn't clear.
- Repeat back to the surgeon the key information you've been given, to clarify you've heard and understood correctly.

It is important to find a healthcare professional you are comfortable talking with about your history. Be honest. Let them know how much you smoke and drink if they ask. Let them know about any street drugs, dietary supplements or any other medicines you're taking or have taken recently.

All the information in this book is a general guide. Your surgeon will give you a clearer, more individual guide to what to expect. It will depend on your health, your recovery and what your job is. A more physically demanding job might require a longer recovery time. You may heal a little faster or slower than average.

Questions and concerns about the surgery can pop into your head at unexpected times, especially as you're falling asleep. In the weeks leading up to your consultation, keep a notebook or a document on your phone with you where you can jot down questions when they come to you.

Going into hospital

Every hospital is a little different, and the experience you have on the day might be different to someone else's. But here is a general description of what happens when you go to hospital.

Arrive at the hospital and follow the instructions you received in the letter or email about when to turn up and which room to go to. You may have the surgery that day or the next. You may get your own room, or you may be on a ward with a curtain you can pull around your bed.

You will have forms to fill in, and you will be asked lots of questions about your medical history.

You will be given a gown to wear that fastens at the back, surgical underwear and surgical stockings. These are very tight socks you wear in order to decrease the chance of getting a blood clot in your legs. Before the operation, the anaesthetist will visit you and ask you some questions.

If you have your own room there may be a television, but not always. Some hospitals have Wi-Fi, but not all of them do. It is a good idea to check with the hospital ahead of time about their policy on using laptops, mobile phones or handheld game consoles. Start by looking at the hospital's website.

Hospital beds usually come with a control pad that moves the bed up and down and a button to call the nurse. It's a good idea to familiarise yourself with this before the surgery so you can use it easily.

All hospitals have visiting times for friends and family, and these can usually be found on the hospital's website or by calling their general enquiries number. You can also ask the nurses on the ward.

It can be disorientating being in hospital, as it's not always clear what you need to do or what will happen next. It can seem confusing who you are supposed to speak to, or to find the right person when you need them. This is normal for being in hospital. Take your time and bring something with you to keep you occupied. There is usually quite a bit of waiting around until it's your turn.

It is not uncommon to have a lot of doubts the night before your surgery or have anxiety when you come round. Sometimes this is just the stress of the situation. It's good to be in contact with friends to talk it through and see if it's just pre-op jitters or a sign that you are not ready. But if you change your mind, you can always leave.

The day of the surgery

Even if you have been looking forward to having surgery, it is still understandable to be nervous on the day, especially if you haven't had surgery or a general anaesthetic before.

You may have been asked to not eat or drink for several hours before the surgery, including sweets or water. This is to ensure you don't throw up when you are given the general anaesthetic. If you take insulin for diabetes, you'll still need to avoid eating and drinking before surgery, but make sure you tell the medical team so appropriate precautions can be taken.

You will need to remove body piercings, make up and nail polish before the surgery, so the doctors can see your skin and nails clearly, and to prevent sources of bacteria coming into the hospital.

While there could well be some pain as you recover from surgery, especially as you start to move around, you should not be in consistent pain. While you're in hospital, if you have a high level of pain or discomfort, call the nurse.

Leaving the hospital

Surgery takes a toll on your body, and while you might be pain free and keen to get right back into life, your body will need time to recover and heal. You will be more tired. For a good recovery, not just for the look of the scars, but for your body to heal inside and out, give yourself time to rest and take it easy, even if you feel fine.

Complications are best dealt with sooner rather than later. When you leave the hospital, ask for the number or email you should use if you are concerned about pain, stitches, swelling, infection, an allergic reaction or anything that just doesn't feel right or you didn't expect.

Before you leave the hospital, take an opportunity to ask the nurses any questions you have about looking after your wound sites. Everyone is slightly different, so how one person recovers, and how long it took them, does not mean it will be the same for you. It's better to listen to your own body and notice how it is recovering.

Questions to ask before you leave the hospital:

- When should I change the dressings?
- How often do I change the dressings?
- When can I take a shower?
- When can I start exercising?
- How do I minimise the size of the scars?
- How often do I take painkillers?
- What should I do if I experience a lot of pain?
- What should I do if I think something is wrong?
- Will I need to come back to the hospital or visit my GP to check the wounds are healing?
- Do I need to have stitches out?
- Is there anything I should look for, such as signs of infection or haematoma?
- How do I get a sick note so I can take time off work or study?

It is likely the hospital will give you some painkillers to take home with you, with instructions. Be sure to check what kind they are and what other painkillers can be taken with them and which can't. Check if they interact with any other medications you're on.

It is a really good idea to have someone with you when you leave the hospital if you can, to help you carry all your bags, to drive you or for general support. When you leave hospital, you will still be sore and find you are moving slowly.

Recovering from surgery can be fun. You get to watch lots of TV, take time off from work and have friends and family take care of you. But it can also be difficult and stressful if you're worried about money, worried about who is taking care of the things you usually take care of, if you don't have a lot of support around you or if you're used to being very active and busy and don't like resting. If that's you, it can be tempting to get back to your usual levels of activity before your body is ready. For the sake of your body healing fully, reducing the risk of complications and reducing the size of scars in the future, take the time to recover.

It is common to feel tearful, depressed or anxious as you get ready to go home after surgery, or over the next few weeks. This might be from the general anaesthetic, or from coming down from the stress and excitement building up to surgery. It can also be stressful and difficult to take care of delicate wound sites and get enough sleep when you're sore and uncomfortable.

General anaesthetic

Most of the surgeries described in this book are performed under general anaesthetic. General anaesthetic is a drug that puts you into a state of controlled unconsciousness so you don't feel any pain while the surgery is carried out.

A general anaesthetic is given as a gas or liquid. You might receive it through a mask over your mouth and nose, or through a cannula, which is a thin tube placed into a vein. The anaesthetic usually works very quickly, within ten or fifteen seconds. An anaesthetist will be beside you throughout the whole operation to ensure you remain comfortable.

It is not clear how anaesthetics work, but it seems that they all interrupt the signals along your nerves so things that would be painful do not get recognised by the brain.

After the operation, the anaesthetist will stop the anaesthetic and you will slowly wake up. A general anaesthetic can affect your memory, concentration and reflexes for twenty-four to forty-eight hours, so it's important to have someone with you after an operation.

If you haven't had a general anaesthetic before, you might not know if you are someone who has a reaction to it. There are some common side effects you might experience, but they do not usually last long. Common side effects are:

- feeling sick or being sick
- shivering and feeling cold
- confusion and memory loss (this is more common in older people)
- problems peeing
- dizziness
- bruising and soreness around the area where you received the general anaesthetic
- sore throat.

When you come round you will probably find it is a bit like waking up from sleep, but it can take longer to feel fully awake.

Some of the surgeries in Chapter 6: Facial Feminisation Surgery can be performed under a local anaesthetic. This is when just one area of your body becomes immune to pain temporarily, but you remain conscious.

Information on surgery and the BMI

BMI stands for body mass index. It is a system medical people use for determining if a person is a healthy weight for their height. It is calculated using the equation:

Your weight in kilograms ÷ Your height in metres

This gives you a number. A "healthy" BMI is said to be between 18 and 30. Some surgical centres require people to have a BMI of under 30 before performing surgery.

But our bodies are individual. While obesity can lead to health risks such as high blood pressure, some people dispute the usefulness of BMI for determining if we are healthy enough to have surgery.

A patient's weight is a concern for surgeons because it can impact on performing the surgery, as well as your recovery afterwards. Carrying a lot of weight can also lead to other health conditions that can affect how well the surgery goes:

- **Sleep apnoea.** Being overweight increases your chance of developing sleep apnoea, a condition that causes you to briefly stop breathing during your sleep. If you have sleep apnoea it can make having a general anaesthetic riskier.
- **High blood pressure.** Being overweight can lead to higher blood pressure. Higher blood pressure puts your surgery at greater risk.

Even if you don't have either of these conditions, carrying a lot of weight can lead to challenges, including:

- locating your veins to give you anaesthesia
- determining the right dose of medications
- making sure you get enough oxygen when you're unconscious
- taking longer to come round from the anaesthesia
- being able to place the breathing tube used while you're unconscious.

It can be very distressing to hear that a surgeon will not perform surgery because of your weight. And it can be extra difficult if you have a history of eating problems or limited mobility.

Losing weight is physically and psychologically difficult. If you are finding weight loss very difficult, and not having the gender confirmation surgery very distressing, discuss this with your surgeon.

A minimum weight can also be a problem for some surgeries, particularly phalloplasty, which requires a certain amount of body fat in order to create a substantial penis shape. But surgeons can recognise that high or low muscle mass can distort BMI, and should give you an individual assessment of your body type.

Giving up smoking

Many of the surgeries in this book will require you to stop smoking several weeks before your surgical date and continue to not smoke afterwards. Stopping smoking is vital if the surgery involves using grafts from different parts of the body. Small blood vessels are important in grafting surgery, and smoking can inflame them. If the small blood vessels are damaged, your new skin graft will not get enough blood and die. Surgeons will not operate if you are still smoking.

Stopping smoking is known to be difficult, but there are a range of options to help. Using just willpower is not as effective as using help like patches, gum and mints and hypnotherapy CDs.

Quitting tips! Once you have picked your quit date, add it to your calendar.

- List your reasons to quit.
- Tell people you're quitting.
- If you have tried to quit before, remember what worked.
- Use stop-smoking aids.
- Have a plan if you are tempted to smoke.
- List your smoking triggers and how to avoid them.
- Keep cravings at bay by keeping busy.
- Exercise away the urge.

Deep vein thrombosis

Before you have surgery, your surgeon will check your risk of developing a deep vein thrombosis, or DVT. People who are in hospital or who have recently had an operation and can't move around much are more at risk for DVT.

A DVT is when a blood clot develops in a vein, usually in the leg. It can be dangerous as sometimes the clot moves into a vein in the lungs, causing a pulmonary embolism.

In hospital you may be given things to help prevent DVT, such as surgical stockings or pumps around your legs to keep the blood moving. It is important to keep up the preventative measures against DVT when you are home again such as:

- moving around a little throughout the day, if you can
- not lying with your legs crossed, as this restricts blood flow
- keeping hydrated
- not smoking if possible
- moving your toes and feet if you have to lie for long periods.

If you have any symptoms of DVT, contact your doctor. Symptoms include:

- throbbing or cramping pain in one leg (usually not both legs)
- swelling in one leg
- warm skin around the painful area
- red or dark skin around the painful area
- swollen veins that are sore when you touch them.

You might also get these symptoms in your arm or tummy if that's where the blood clot is.[1]

---

1   NHS (2023). DVT. www.nhs.uk/conditions/deep-vein-thrombosis-dvt

Before going into hospital checklist

- ☐ Created a surgery budget.
- ☐ Organised time off work or studying.
- ☐ Given up or cut down smoking.
- ☐ Stocked house with food for when you come home.
- ☐ Organised things to keep you distracted and entertained while you're in hospital.
- ☐ Got comfy, easy-to-wear clothes for hospital and at home.
- ☐ Arranged for someone to take you and pick you up when you're discharged.
- ☐ Organised pet care or childcare.
- ☐ Got your bedroom set up so you can move around easily.

Leaving the hospital checklist

- ☐ Got your sick note for time off work or studying.
- ☐ Got your medications and medical supplies.
- ☐ Got all your bags, phone and everything you brought with you.
- ☐ Got answers to all your questions.
- ☐ Know who to call or email if you're worried about any of the surgical sites.
- ☐ Know when your next appointment is for a wound check.
- ☐ Know how to take care of your surgical sites.

13

Fertility, Contraception and Having a Baby

There are few studies on trans people and parenting, but all conclude around 50 per cent of trans people want to have children.[1] And while there is little information on it, there is no evidence that having a transgender parent causes any harm to a child. But these studies also suggest people don't want to delay their transition, or add to the cost, by arranging fertility options for the future. Some surgeries will remove your options around having children using your own eggs or sperm, so this chapter looks at your options around storing eggs or sperm.

For people born with a uterus
Contraception
Taking testosterone is not a contraceptive, and there have been trans men on testosterone who have unexpectedly got pregnant. An absence of periods (amenorrhoea) does not mean a person has stopped ovulating. If you are taking testosterone and do get pregnant, testosterone can damage the foetus.

Condoms are the most effective way to prevent both pregnancy

---

1 Bouman, W.P. (2017). *Transgender Handbook: A Guide for Transgender People, Their Families and Professionals.* Hauppauge, NY: Nova Science Publishers, Inc.

and sexually transmitted infections (STIs). They are effective 98 per cent of the time when used correctly. Other options to prevent pregnancy are a progesterone-only medication or a progesterone intrauterine device. Testosterone is not known to interfere with a hormonal-based method of contraception. Sub-dermal implants may also be a good option as they are the most effective contraception for people with ovaries, they don't require a pelvic procedure and they can be easily concealed. Implants can also have androgenic activity, meaning they increase "male" characteristics.

No hormones are male or female. Everyone produces both testosterone and oestrogen, but in different quantities and in different regions of their body. While in cisgender men testosterone is known to improve sexual desire, one study found if their oestrogen is inhibited, the sexual desire is reduced, suggesting both testosterone and oestrogen have a role in sexual desire.[2] In cisgender women also, both oestrogen and testosterone appear to have a role in sexual desire.

A copper IUD may be an option if a hormonal contraceptive device aggravates dysphoria, though it is unknown if taking testosterone makes any difference to its effectiveness.

If you want to get pregnant

Trans people who have been on testosterone and had top surgery can get pregnant and deliver a baby vaginally. If you think delivering a baby yourself is something you'll be interested in doing in the future, this can have an impact on your choices around lower surgery.

If you have been taking testosterone and your periods have stopped (before menopause), they will start again if you stop taking testosterone. The ovarian follicles – the number of eggs you have available for pregnancy – will not have been reduced.

While it is possible to keep your vagina with metoidioplasty, it is not recommended to deliver a baby after lower surgery.

---

2   Holmberg, M., Arver, S. and Dhejne, C. (2019). Supporting sexuality and improving sexual function in transgender persons. *Nature Reviews Urology*, 16, 121–139. https://doi.org/10.1038/s41585-018-0108-8

Being pregnant is still an option. If you keep your uterus, carrying a baby to term and then having a caesarean section is still possible.

If pregnancy is one of the factors you are considering, then include this in your personal timeline (see Chapter 8: Metoidioplasty for more information on building your personal timeline).

There are now several trans men and non-binary people who have given birth and documented the process. You can hear about their stories here:

- BBC podcast Pride & Joy
- Seahorse documentary.

Preserving fertility for later use

If you want to have children in the future that are genetically related to you, but don't want to get pregnant yourself, there are a few different options for extracting and storing your eggs. The eggs can then be fertilised and implanted into a surrogate. If you take testosterone, it is recommended to either have your eggs extracted prior to starting taking testosterone or stopping testosterone before extraction. A three-month period of being off testosterone is advised.

Options for fertility preservation

Oocyte cryopreservation

Hormones are used to stimulate the ovaries to produce more eggs than usual. The eggs are then extracted, frozen and stored in a laboratory. The eggs can then be thawed, fertilised to become an embryo and then put inside a uterus. An embryo is the stage of human development for the first seven weeks. The process requires frequent vaginal ultrasound monitoring, using a probe inside the vagina, which can be psychologically difficult for some trans people.

Embryo cryopreservation

This involves the same process as oocyte cryopreservation, but the eggs are fertilised before they are frozen. This is known as in vitro fertilisation. The embryos can then be later thawed and put back inside a uterus. The embryos can be stored, frozen, for around ten years. The length of time they are frozen does not affect how likely they are to lead to pregnancy. This is also called embryo banking and embryo freezing.

Ovarian tissue cryopreservation
This process does not require ovarian stimulation via hormones. Under anaesthesia, small pieces of ovarian tissue are removed and frozen. Later, they can be returned to your body close to where they were taken. Once they have been returned, ovarian activity will resume, and you can get pregnant in the normal way.

For embryo and oocyte cryopreservation, the age of the donor is important for success.

For people born with a penis
Contraception
Taking oestrogen only partially suppresses sperm production, and so it is still possible to get someone pregnant even if you have been taking oestrogen. It is not a contraceptive.

Condoms are useful for preventing both STIs and pregnancy, so long as they are fitted correctly. If you're taking oestrogen it can cause your penis to shrink and produce smaller erections, so a smaller condom size might be needed.

Another option is to have a vasectomy, as this does not interfere with hormones (and is somewhat reversible).

If you want to get someone pregnant
If you want to get someone pregnant, you will have a greater chance if you temporarily stop taking oestrogen. The effect of oestrogen on how much sperm you produce is reversible, after around three to seven months of stopping hormones.

Preserving fertility for later use

If you are going to bank sperm, you may need to reduce your hormones temporarily.

Options for fertility preservation

Sperm cryopreservation

This is the simplest and most reliable method. Once the sperm are released from the testicles (usually through masturbation) they can be frozen and stored a long time. The longest successful storage is forty years.

Surgical sperm extraction

This process uses a needle to extract sperm from the testicle. It can be a good option if masturbation is difficult or distressing.

> *I'd done my research before I started on hormones. I was 18, and my parents didn't know. I spent probably $2500 or $3000 on cryo-preservation and semen analysis tests to make sure everything was good to go with the initial specimen collections. I did three of them. I only needed to do one, but I really want kids, and I had to ensure that was going to happen.*
>
> Mikey

14

Scars

Scars are inevitable after surgery. They can be large or hidden, depending on what surgery you have and how you heal. Surgeons will aim to minimise scars by placing them in specific locations.

Scars are made from fibrous tissue; they replace normal tissue when there has been an injury. No two scars will heal the same, but generally scars will appear red and raised at first and usually become paler and smoother over time. It usually takes one to two years for a scar to fully settle.

Different skin tones can scar differently. White skin can scar leaving either lighter or darker tones than the surrounding skin. Darker scars can fade to white over time, whereas lighter scars do not darken. Black and brown skin can also produce scar lines that are darker or lighter than the surrounding skin.

When you first leave hospital, and in the first weeks afterwards, your incisions will need to heal. Your main job at this time is keep them clean and dry and minimise how much you pull on the skin around the area. Once the scars have healed, you may find they are still very visible, but this will continue to change and they will minimise over the years. There are some things you can still do over the years to help your scars reduce in size and colour:

- After surgery you may be asked to keep your wound dry for some time. Once you can shower or bathe again, wash your scars gently; don't scrub them or pick at the scabs. Pat them dry.

- Skin around the scar can become tight. Try using a moisturiser such as E45 cream or an aqueous cream on the skin around the scar to keep it supple.
- Smoking can delay the healing process. If you can, give up smoking during your recovery.
- You can also use a topical silicone gel or silicone gel sheets or pressure dressings to help improve the appearance of a scar.

Every year the scars changed a little bit more. They took a few years to fade to white, and even after five years they were still changing, becoming flatter, evening out.

Edward

Keloid scars

Sometimes a scar will become larger, thicker and raised up. This happens when the body produces too much collagen around the wound. This is called a keloid scar. Sometimes keloid scars can be itchy and painful.

Anyone can get a keloid scar, but they are more common in people with darker skin, such as people from Africa and African-Caribbean and south Indian communities.

It's not known what causes keloid scars, but if you have one it is more likely you'll develop another. Keloid scars sometimes don't form until several months or years after the original wound.

There are treatments for keloid scars if you are bothered by them, but they are not always successful. Treatments include:

- steroid injections
- steroid-impregnated tape
- silicone gel sheeting
- freezing early keloid scars with liquid nitrogen to stop them growing
- laser treatment to reduce redness
- surgery, sometimes followed by radiotherapy, to remove

the scar (although it can grow back and may be larger than before).

Sunscreen

Scars are sensitive to strong sunlight, so always wear sunscreen in the future. The NHS advises a sunscreen of factor 30 or higher for the first eighteen months after surgery when your scar is uncovered in the sun. The American Academy of Dermatology recommends using a sunscreen that is broad spectrum, at least factor 30 and water resistant, as well as using shade and sun protective clothing when possible.

15

Sex

Sex is normal

If you want sex, if you don't want sex, if you're not sure what you want, that is all normal and okay.

We can all feel pressure to have sex by a certain age, in a certain way. Messages about what sex is, and what we should want, are everywhere. It can be hard to hear and trust your own voice if it's telling you something different to all those other messages.

A lot of focus gets given to "penis in vagina" sex, which can give the impression that unless you want that, there is something wrong or odd about you. This isn't true. So long as it is consensual, you can have sex any way you want, including choosing not to have sex or masturbate at all.

All this is true for cisgender people just as much as for trans and non-binary people. But trans and non-binary people get a lot of extra messages about how we should feel about our bodies and how we should feel about having sex with our bodies.

It is common for trans and non-binary people to feel uncomfortable in their bodies, before, during or after transitioning. And it is common for trans and non-binary people to find sex and intimacy difficult because of this. For example, one study found only 50 per cent of trans people with a partner were using their genitals.[1]

This chapter looks at sexual orientation, how broad it is and

---

1   Mancini, I., Alvisi, S., Gava, G., Seracchioli, R. and Meriggiola, M.C. (2020). Contraception across transgender. *International Journal of Impotence Research, 33*(7), 710–719. https://doi.org/10.1038/s41443-021-00412-z

how transitioning can impact on it. It also looks at how trans and non-binary people feel about sex before, during and after transition and how to navigate that.

Sexual orientation

Sexual orientation refers to who you feel attracted to for sexual stuff. Sexual stuff doesn't mean penetration, or being naked or having someone else touch your genitals. Those are things you might do, but they're not essentials. Your sexual orientation is your own. It's what makes you aroused. That's really a *you-know-it-when-you-feel-it* thing.

Sexual orientation is a broad spectrum. We have terms that describe the general areas, but often people do not fit exactly into any category. These are some of the most common terms:

- **Lesbian.** Someone who identifies as a woman and is sexually attracted to women. Some people describe themselves as "gay women".
- **Gay man.** Someone who identifies as a man and is sexually attracted to men.
- **Bisexual or bi.** Someone who is sexually attracted to men and women. As understanding of gender has expanded, bi often means being attracted to people of all genders. Some people prefer the term pansexual to mean attracted to people of all genders.
- **Asexual.** Sometimes also referred to as "ace". Someone who doesn't have sexual attraction to other people, or very little. Like other terms, it is a spectrum. People who identify as asexual can experience a range of feelings. Some have romantic feelings, some don't.
- **Queer.** Queer is a broad term. It encompasses a wide range of identities, both gender and sexual. It generally means not straight or not cisgender, but how people interpret it can be individual.
- **Straight/heterosexual.** Someone who is attracted to people with a different gender identity to them.

People don't always fit neatly into different categories; some people are "mostly straight" but not all the time, or bi but mostly into men. You might also have romantic feelings for someone without having any sexual attraction. People can be along a spectrum for sexual feelings and along a different one for romantic feelings.

Everyone's experience is unique, and none is better than others.

Sex and transitioning

Hormone therapy and gender confirmation surgery can affect your interest in sex, or your sexual activity. However, body image, self-esteem, your general well-being and sexual anxiety are also important elements to your overall sexual satisfaction. Hormones and surgery can improve your gender dysphoria, but they may not solve all problems of body image and anxiety. Relationships can be difficult if you choose to tell someone about your trans identity.

Some people do report that their sexual orientation changes as they transition. This might mean either being attracted to a gender they never have before, or their preference for one over another increasing or decreasing. This experience has not been well studied, so it is not clear exactly why some people experience this.

Of course, just the process of transitioning can alter the label of your identity, even if your internal preferences haven't changed.

If you take hormones, this can change your sexual feelings. Some people report testosterone increasing their sex drive (libido), but others report no change or their libido going down. Oestrogen can make the penis and testicles shrink, and this might change how you have sex. Some people find oestrogen causes a decrease in sexual desire, while others find no change or an increase. So the experiences are varied, and other factors can have an individual impact. Some trans women find their sexual desire goes down too low. This can be improved with low doses of testosterone that bring their testosterone levels into a range more in line with the experience of a cisgender woman.

One effect of oestrogen was how I would now orgasm. I play with the end, kind of just rub it whereas before I'd do more like stroking, and the orgasm is different. I can keep going, it's much more of a mental one, I have to be on it, whereas before I didn't. Before I'd describe like the best sneeze ever, much quicker.

That's another thing that's interesting for me, I'm not inhibited to self-pleasure; I'm not repulsed, though my body's not where I want it to be. I have friends who have a disconnect or awkwardness with their body, and probably the worst time to have a disconnect with your body is when you're trying to be sexually pleasured. It's important to try to learn acceptance of your body and feel okay and know someone could love you and your body when you're not happy with it.

Maya

Taking testosterone can reduce vaginal lubrication and thin the lining of the vagina. If you like to use your vagina for sex, you may find using extra lube makes it more comfortable.

While gender confirming treatment can improve body satisfaction overall, there can be a period during the early stages where gender dysphoria gets worse. This might be because the gender dysphoria was buried as a coping strategy, whereas the process of speaking openly about your trans identity and addressing issues with medical practitioners makes denial no longer an option. It brings everything to the surface.

I was kind of hoping that I would miraculously be more comfortable with sex, and I'm not. Better than I was, but I'm not. It is quite nice to be able to fuck somebody and feel it, which never was something I thought interested me, but it does feel pretty good. I just don't think I'm a particularly sexual person. I like the idea, I like the theory, but in practice it's just all a bit awkward. That didn't change like I hoped it would.

Bryn, talking about having metoidioplasty

Getting comfortable with sex

Whether you choose to have surgery or not, you may find your
feelings about sex change as you transition. It's not uncommon
for people to be uncomfortable with sexual contact, or just
talking about sex, when they are feeling gender dysphoric. Of
course, you can choose to just not have any sexual contact until
you feel more comfortable. It can be difficult, though, to manage
both having a libido and having gender dysphoria. And of course,
feeling uncomfortable in your body is not unique to trans people.
There could be all kinds of reasons someone finds sex difficult.

Sex doesn't have to be with another person around. Masturbation is normal and a great way to get sexual contact in your
life without having to involve anyone else. Masturbation is still a
taboo subject for a lot of people and connected to a lot of shame.
But it's your body, and there is nothing wrong with it.

Here are some ideas for how to manage sexual contact with
another person while at times having gender dysphoric feelings.
There is no right answer and these ideas might not work for you;
you're not doing anything wrong if you still find it hard. Sometimes, gender dysphoria is just hard.

- Be clear with your partner what you want and don't want.
  The anxiety of your partner doing something that triggers
  your gender dysphoria can be distracting. Being clear
  with your partner(s) about what you like and don't like is
  a good idea anyway, but it is extra important if something
  could cause you distress. Sometimes these conversations
  are difficult and upsetting to have, so pick the time that
  works for you.
- Use different language for the body parts you find triggering if you find it helps.
- Keep any clothes on you want. Sex doesn't mean naked.
  If keeping all or some of your clothes on makes you comfortable, no problem! Maybe you want to keep your underwear on, keep your binder on or keep yourself tucked. You
  might have an outfit that is comfortable just for sex.
- If you aren't comfortable with your partner(s) touching a

certain part or parts of your body, you can touch it yourself. You don't have to be touched anywhere you don't want to be.

- Have sex when you want, how often you want. If sex is something you enjoy but also find difficult, you might find you need a break between sessions to process the difficult feelings. This might mean sex once a month or every six months – whatever break you need.
- Don't want to be in the same room with someone? Online, phone, email or text sex is all available. It could be with your partners or could be anonymous.
- Toys are handy. If you don't want your partner's hand or hands on your genitals, some people find a toy a useful intermediary. It allows them to give you sexual pleasure without directly touching your body. Toys are available for vaginas, clitorises and penises. There are also just non-specific vibrating toys that feel nice against erogenous zones.
- You don't have to be spontaneous. Spontaneous sex might not work for you if you need to do a bit of mental preparation, or physical prep, like getting the right underwear on.
- Use the language that works and avoid the words that don't.
- It's not all about orgasm. If you enjoy sex with your partners but find it hard to orgasm, that's not a reason to abandon doing the stuff you do like.
- Sex doesn't have to be symmetrical. You don't have to do the exact same things to each other. If you have a partner who likes to be naked and you don't, that's okay.
- And finally – worth saying again – be clear with your partner(s). All these suggestions have a built-in clause – let them know what you like and what you don't.

I definitely felt more comfortable having sex with men after top surgery, 'cause I felt more of a man in lots of different ways. I remember having a BDSM hook-up with this guy a couple of months before I started taking testosterone. Although he said he understood my identity, he still managed to misgender me at some point and it was really upsetting obviously.

I think top surgery made a difference; even though I still feel shame around my genitals at times and kind of not man enough because of that, I feel at least if my top half is male looking then it gives me a bit more currency. It helped me feel I could open the door to having sex with men, and in all fairness it did open the door to having sex with men because I think I was much more accepted.

Over the years my sexuality has changed a bit. That's partly because I feel more comfortable in my body and more comfortable to seek out the things I desire. I feel like I've got more of a pass to seek out things I deserve. I remember pre-top surgery looking through books of Tom of Finland with a friend and thinking the pictures look so cool, so amazing, I wish I could look like that. And then I find myself ten years later, a leatherman in a leather club. I'm like, what happened? I didn't need lower surgery for that. That was testosterone and top surgery and a lot of journey along the way.

Finn

Consent

Consent means being free and able to give an emphatic yes to the sex you want, with who you want and when you want. If you are unconscious, asleep, have taken drugs or are drunk, you are not able to give consent. Likewise, you are responsible for your partners being able to give consent.

Your partners might find having sex in a different way to what they're used to difficult at first, and adjusting to what works for both them and you might take some practice and getting used to. This is normal. But you don't have to put up with any behaviour that puts pressure on you or tries to manipulate you. The following are red flags that you don't have to put up with:

- Your partner saying if you loved them you'd have sex more often.

- Your partner saying other trans and non-binary people get over their sexual problems.
- Your partner suggesting you should "get over the dysphoria" by going to therapy.
- Your partner complaining you are making them feel unsexy or unattractive.
- Your partner behaving passive aggressively around sex, such as saying "it's fine" if you don't want sex this week, but then acting cold, distant or argumentative.
- Your partner listening to your preferences for "no go" areas but then going there and saying they were "just caught up in the moment".
- Your partner saying they have to do certain things to show you they love you.
- Your partner saying they will leave you or have sex with other people if they don't get the sex they want.

16

Sexual Health and Check-Ups

Sexual health

Whatever parts of the body you have, it's a good idea to keep an eye on them. Get to know the signs and symptoms to look out for that indicate there might be something wrong.

If you have anything that doesn't seem right with your genitals, such as rashes, warts, smells, discharge or pain, including pain or stinging when you pee, visit a sexual health clinic. Sexual health clinics, also sometimes called GUM clinics (genito-urinary clinics), are places to get tested for sexual transmitted infections, including HIV, and for information about safer sex. Depending on where you live, you might be able to get free condoms and lube.

Going to a sexual health clinic can make anyone feel embarrassed. Sometimes you can take your own swabs for tests, which can be helpful if you find showing your body to a nurse difficult. Some sexual health clinics have set times for trans and non-binary people, but others will not, and some may not have much experience with trans and non-binary people.

General sexual health tips:

- Use a condom on penises or toys used for penetration.
- Lube is good for helping with penetration. Use water based rather than oil based. Oil-based lubes can damage condoms, making them less effective.
- If you have had a vaginoplasty, dilating before sex can help

stretch the vagina a little so it's more comfortable, but it can cause small tears and bleeding that increase the risk of STIs.

- If you've had a phalloplasty, the inside of the penis is different to the inside of a natal penis. But you can still catch STIs if you have penetrative sex without a condom.
- You are more at risk of catching an STI when you are still recovering from surgery because there is a greater risk of bleeding around the genitals.

Smear tests

A smear test is a test to check the health of the cervix, the opening to the uterus. It is not a test for cancer, but rather to prevent cancer. They can also be called pap smears or cervical screenings. The tests are recommended for people between the age of 25 and 65.

The test involves taking a sample of your cells to test for human papilloma virus (HPV). This virus can cause changes to the cells of the cervix. The test involves a hollow tube (a speculum) being inserted into the vagina, and then a brush being used to collect cells from the cervix. Speculums come in different sizes, so if one is uncomfortable, you can ask for a smaller one.

You are still at risk for cervical cancer if:

- you have had the HPV vaccine – it does not protect you from all types of HPV
- you have only had one sexual partner
- you have had the same partner, or not had sex, for a long time – you can have HPV for a long time without knowing it
- you're a lesbian or bisexual – you can get HPV from any sexual contact
- you have had a partial hysterectomy – not all hysterectomies remove the cervix.

Testosterone is not known to increase the risk of cervical cancer. It is common for trans men and non-binary people to be uncomfortable having smear tests. Some are, some aren't. If you have a cervix, they are an important test to have. As mentioned, some cities have clinics where there are sessions especially for trans and non-binary people to have sexual health tests, so it may be worth seeking out one of those clinics if you feel uncomfortable.

If you have changed your gender marker (whether you're registered as male or female) at a clinic or GP, you may not get automatic reminders to come in for a smear test. Different clinics work differently. Speak with your clinic or GP about what their system is for trans patients.

Ovarian cancer

Anyone who has ovaries can get ovarian cancer, but it mostly affects people over 50. The symptoms include frequently experiencing:

- a swollen tummy or feeling bloated
- pain or tenderness in your tummy or the area between the hips (pelvis)
- no appetite or feeling full quickly after eating
- an urgent need to pee or needing to pee more often.

Other symptoms of ovarian cancer can include:

- indigestion
- constipation or diarrhoea
- back pain
- feeling tired all the time
- losing weight without trying
- bleeding from the vagina that is not a period.

If you have symptoms, go to your GP and they will need to examine you. The exam will involve undressing from the waist down and lying on a bench so they can look at your vagina. The doctor will need to put a speculum into your vagina so they can see inside. You can ask the doctor to stop at any time. There is no link between taking testosterone and developing ovarian cancer.

Uterus cancer

Anyone who has a uterus can get uterus cancer. The main symptoms of uterus cancer include:

- heavy periods from your vagina that are unusual for you
- vaginal bleeding between your periods
- a change to your vaginal discharge.

Other symptoms of uterus cancer can include:

- a lump or swelling in your tummy or between your hip bones (pelvis)
- pain in your lower back or between your hip bones (pelvis)
- pain during sex
- blood in your pee.

Cancer of the vulva is rare, and it mostly affects people over the age of 65. Cancer of the fallopian tubes is also rare.

Prostate health

The prostate is not removed as part of lower surgery for trans women and non-binary people, so screening for prostate cancer, especially in older patients, is still required. If you have a prostate, here's more information about it and some signs it might be unhealthy.

The prostate is a gland that only people born with a penis have. A gland is an organ that produces a substance e.g. milk, tears, sweat or hormones. It is about the size of a walnut, and it sits in a ring around the urethra, just below the bladder. It produces a thick, white fluid that when mixed with sperm creates semen.

The prostate tends to get swollen as you get over the age of 50, and this can lead to some problems. It's not clear why it gets swollen. Sometimes it gets bigger due to prostatitis or prostate cancer. When the prostate gets swollen, it can put pressure on the urethra making it difficult to start peeing, or causing pain when you pee. See your GP if you have these symptoms.

Prostate cancer is the most common form of cancer for people with a prostate. It mainly affects people over the age of 65, though people over 50 are at risk. You may also be more at risk if you have a close family member who has had prostate cancer, or a close family member who has had breast cancer. Black people are more at risk than white people.

If you have any of these symptoms, see your GP:

- difficulty starting or stopping urinating
- a weak flow of urine
- straining when peeing
- feeling like you're not able to fully empty your bladder
- prolonged dribbling after you've finished peeing
- needing to pee more frequently or more suddenly
- waking up frequently during the night to pee.

See your GP if you notice any problems with, or changes to, your usual pattern of urination.

No one likes going to the doctor or nurse if there is something wrong with their genitals or bum. Absolutely no one. But doctors and nurses have seen bodies of all types and are often unfazed. Connect with other trans people in your area to find information about which clinics and doctors they have had a good experience with.

One Final Thing

This book has covered a lot of information, but it could never answer all your questions or prepare you for every complication or unexpected thing. If you still have lots of questions, that's good. I encourage you to ask your surgeon lots of questions. Seek out other trans and non-binary people, and ask them lots of questions too.

It can feel overwhelming. It's okay to find the information confusing. It's definitely okay to be angry or upset that you are expected to do all this research just to get to a place where you feel like yourself. I get that.

Here are a few final words from some of the people I spoke to:

Don't rush. For people early on in transition, your concept of what you will want can change. If you do not have horrible dysphoria, and you're actually just not sure, take time. I absolutely understand that for some people everything needs to be done as quickly as possible and that's the only way they can survive. But I'm glad I took ten years to decide. Even before I had started on hormones I had figured that if I did have surgery it would be meta, but it gave me plenty of time to really think, did I need to or was it just because I was expected to? It gave me time to make the right decision for me.

Bryn

Don't just listen to other trans people but listen to your surgeon. You can go in with preconceived ideas. Work with your surgeon for what's best for your body. Immediate results are not what you should look at; you have to wait years for the real results to come through.

Finn

For people having vaginoplasty, definitely go to a pelvic floor therapist, and never cease your dilation. Because the moment you skip one, the next one will be even worse. Find a community of people who have been through it before you. Ask your doctor if they can put you in touch with anyone.

Mikey

Be realistic about what the end result will be, and that you might have revisions, and how it will look. Try to find information that's digestible, whether that's text or images. Look at the results that are from six months later or longer and find out how people have coped and what's happened with the complications. Try to be realistic about it all.

Maya

If your kid comes out as trans, whether or not it's a phase, whether or not they want to do something with their gender in the future: this isn't weird. They're not going to have a weird life, they're not a weird kid, they're normal.

Jon

Giving a fuck is the biggest problem I think. So if I can give anyone advice it's just follow your heart, try to find what best suits your body.

Sonia

I am passionate about a future in which trans people are not pressured to feel their body has to be a certain way, that they must cleave to a template based on cisgender bodies – which, of course, are endlessly variable themselves! I expect a good chunk of trans people will always see their goal as "blending in", and I hope there will be ever-better surgeries to help them achieve that aim. I hope we're moving to a world where trans people can be confident about making decisions that reflect what they genuinely want for themselves and that aren't being governed by the expectations of others, whether of society as a whole or the doctors we have to negotiate with on these pathways.

Inés

Bibliography

The Basics

Effects of Different Steps in Gender Reassignment Therapy on Psychopathology: A Prospective Study of Persons with a Gender Identity Disorder. www.sciencedirect.com/science/article/abs/pii/S1743609515305336

General Anaesthesia. www.nhs.uk/conditions/general-anaesthesia

Getting Back to Normal. www.nhs.uk/conditions/having-surgery/recovery

Plemons, E. (2017). *The Look of a Woman*. Durham, NC: Duke University Press Books.

Preparation for Surgery. https://thrive.kaiserpermanente.org/care-near-you/northern-california/eastbay/wp-content/uploads/sites/6/2020/04/Metoidioplasty-and-Phalloplasty-Surgery-Preparation.pdf

Problem Solving. www.psychologytools.com/resource/problem-solving

Reconstructive Management Pearls for the Transgender Patient. https://link.springer.com/article/10.1007/s11934-018-0795-y

Think Over Before You Make Over. www.bapras.org.uk/public/think-over-before-you-make-over; www.bapras.org.uk/docs/default-source/thinkover/baprasthinkoverguide_final.pdf?sfvrsn=2

Transbucket. transbucket.com

Understanding How Risk Is Discussed in Health Care – Patient Information Leaflet. www.rcog.org.uk/for-the-public/browse-all-patient-information-leaflets/understanding-how-risk-is-discussed-in-health-care

Which Countries Recognize Third Gender Option on Passports? www.newsweek.com/which-countries-recognize-third-gender-option-passports-1643167

Thinking about Surgery

A Guide to Feminizing Hormones. www.seattlechildrens.org/pdf/PE2706.pdf

Considering Cosmetic Surgery? www.bapras.org.uk/public/patient-information/cosmetic-surgery/considering-cosmetic-surgery

Breast Augmentation

ALCL and Breast Implants. www.bapras.org.uk/public/patient-information/patient-advice-and-guidelines/alcl-and-breast-implants

Breast Augmentation Fact Sheet. https://baaps.org.uk/_userfiles/pages/files/breast_augmentation_fact_sheet.pdf

Breast Augmentation for Transfeminine Patients: Methods, Complications, and Outcomes. https://gs.amegroups.com/article/view/38543/html

Breast Development in Transwomen after 1 Year of Cross-Sex Hormone Therapy: Results of a Prospective Multicenter Study. https://academic.oup.com/jccm/article/103/2/532/4642966

Breast Enlargement (Implants). www.nhs.uk/conditions/cosmetic-procedures/breast-enlargement

Breast Screening (Mammogram). www.nhs.uk/conditions/breast-cancer-screening

Care Quality Commission. www.cqc.org.uk

Choosing Cosmetic Surgery. www.cqc.org.uk/help-advice/help-choosing-care-services/choosing-cosmetic-surgery

Choosing Who Will Do Your Cosmetic Procedure. www.nhs.uk/conditions/cosmetic-procedures/choosing-who-will-do-your-procedure

Federation of State Medical Boards. www.fsmb.org

General Medical Council. www.gmc-uk.org

Good Practice Guidelines for the Assessment and Treatment of Adults with Gender Dysphoria. https://baaps.org.uk/_userfiles/pages/files/print_bapras_breast_aug_2021_final_revised_3.pdf

I'm Trans or Non-Binary, Does This Affect My Cancer Screening? www.cancerresearchuk.org/about-cancer/cancer-symptoms/spot-cancer-early/screening/trans-and-non-binary-cancer-screening#screening50

Information about BIA-ALCL for People with Breast Implants. www.gov.uk/government/publications/information-about-bia-alcl-for-people-with-breast-implants

Key Statistics for Breast Cancer in Men. www.cancer.org/cancer/breast-cancer-in-men/about/key-statistics.html

Long-Term Safety of Textured and Smooth Breast Implants. https://academic.oup.com/asj/article/38/1/38/4259312

Male to Female Gender Affirmation Surgery: Breast Augmentation with Ergonmix Round Protheses. https://pubmed.ncbi.nlm.nih.gov/33723376

The Male Breasts. www.macmillan.org.uk/cancer-information-and-support/breast-cancer/the-male-breasts

Risks and Complications of Breast Implants. www.fda.gov/medical-devices/breast-implants/risks-and-complications-breast-implants

Round Versus Anatomical Implants in Primary Cosmetic Breast Augmentation: A Meta-Analysis and Systematic Review. https://journals.lww.com/plasreconsurg/Abstract/2019/03000/Round_versus_Anatomical_Implants_in_Primary.12.aspx

Scars. www.nhs.uk/conditions/scars

Statement from the Chair of the PRASEAG – 4 April 2019. Risk to People with Breast Implants of Developing a Very Rare Form of Cancer. https://assets.publishing.service.gov.uk/government/uploads/system/uploads/attachment_data/file/793014/Chair_of_the_PRASEAG_statement_FINAL.pdf

Types of Breast Implants. www.fda.gov/medical-devices/breast-implants/types-breast-implants

What Is Breast Cancer Screening? www.cdc.gov/cancer/breast/basic_info/screening.htm

What to Know about Breast Implants. www.fda.gov/consumers/consumer-updates/what-know-about-breast-implants

Your Guide to Breast Augmentation. www.bapras.org.uk/docs/default-source/Patient-Information-Booklets/rcs_bapras_guide_breast_augmentation.pdf?sfvrsn=4

Chest Reconstruction

After Surgery. www.nhs.uk/conditions/having-surgery/afterwards

Breast and Reproductive Cancers in the Transgender Population: A Systematic Review. https://obgyn.onlinelibrary.wiley.com/doi/abs/10.1111/1471-0528.15258

Health Impact of Chest Binding among Transgender Adults: A Community-Engaged, Cross-Sectional Study. www.tandfonline.com/doi/full/10.1080/13691058.2016.1191675

Hormone Management of Trans Men. https://wchh.onlinelibrary.wiley.com/doi/epdf/10.1002/tre.651

How Should I Check My Breasts? www.nhs.uk/common-health-questions/womens-health/how-should-i-check-my-breasts

How to Treat Scars on Black Skin. www.medicalnewstoday.com/articles/scars-on-black-skin

Testosterone Therapy and Risk of Breast Cancer Development: A Systematic Review. https://journals.lww.com/co-urology/Abstract/2020/05000/Testosterone_therapy_and_risk_of_breast_cancer.11.aspx

Vincent, B. (2018). *Transgender Health: A Practitioner's Guide to Binary and Nonbinary Trans Patient Care.* London: Jessica Kingsley Publishers.

What Is Gynaecomastia? www.nhs.uk/common-health-questions/mens-health/what-is-gynaecomastia

WPATH Standards of Care Version 8. www.wpath.org/soc8/chapters

Hysterectomy

After Surgery. www.nhs.uk/conditions/having-surgery/afterwards

Colpocleisis. www.bsuh.nhs.uk/documents/colpocleisis

Complications: Hysterectomy. www.nhs.uk/conditions/hysterectomy/risks/

Hysterectomy for the Transgender Man. https://link.springer.com/article/10.1007/s13669-017-0211-5

LeFort Split Screen Model. www.youtube.com/watch?v=IRcyStA8fPA&ab_channel=AndreyPetrikovetsMDFACOG

Overview: Hysterectomy. www.nhs.uk/conditions/hysterectomy

Sources of Estrogen and Their Importance. https://pubmed.ncbi.nlm.nih.gov/14623515

The Uterus in Transgender Men. www.sciencedirect.com/science/article/abs/pii/S0015028221005811

Facial Feminisation Surgery

Deschamps-Braly, J. and Ousterhout, D.K. (2021). *Facial Feminisation Surgery.* Omaha, NE: Addicus Books.

Facial Feminization Surgery. www.youtube.com/watch?v=djqPzShX0i4&ab_channel=NorthwellHealth

Facial Feminization Surgery Changes Perception of Patient Gender. https://academic.oup.com/asj/article/40/7/703/5611081

Gender-Affirming Hormone Treatment Induces Facial Feminization in Transwomen and Masculinization in Transmen: Quantification by 3D Scanning and Patient-Reported Outcome Measures. www.jsm.jsexmed.org/article/S1743-6095(19)30413-8/fulltext

Gender, Ethnicity, and Transgender Embodiment: Interrogating Classification in Facial Feminization Surgery. https://journals.sagepub.com/doi/10.1177/1357034X18812942

Jaw Reduction Surgery. https://www.sciencedirect.com/science/article/abs/pii/S0030666522000408?via%3Dihub

Rhinoplasty. www.bapras.org.uk/public/patient-information/surgery-guides/rhinoplasty

Rhinoplasty (Augmentation). https://baaps.org.uk/patients/procedures/13/rhinoplasty_augmentation

Lower Surgery for Trans Men and Non-Binary People

Marci L. Bowers, M.D. https://marcibowers.com

Phalloplasty: Techniques and Outcomes. https://tau.amegroups.com/article/view/26419/24265

Vaginectomy. www.sciencedirect.com/topics/medicine-and-dentistry/vaginectomy

Testicular Prosthesis. https://my.clevelandclinic.org/health/treatments/15993-testicular-prosthesis

What Is Metoidioplasty? www.childrenshospital.org/conditions-and-treatments/treatments/metoidioplasty

Metoidioplasty

Age of Majority. https://fra.europa.eu/en/publication/2017/mapping-minimum-age-requirements/age-majority

Anatomy, Histology, and Nerve Density of Clitoris and Associated Structures: Clinical Applications to Vulvar Surgery. www.ajog.org/article/S0002-9378 19)30844-0/fulltext

Genital Gender Affirming Surgery: Masculinizing Surgery with Metoidioplasty. www.youtube.com/watch?v=uA5iYrOzVyw&ab_channel=UCLAHealth

Is Clitoral Release Another Term for Metoidioplasty? A Systematic Review and Meta-Analysis of Metoidioplasty Surgical Technique and Outcomes. www.smoa.jsexmed.org/article/S2050-1161(20)30181-1/fulltext

Living with Urinary Catheter. www.nhs.uk/conditions/urinary-catheters/living-with

Metoidioplasty as a One-Stage Phallic Reconstruction in Transmen. https://parjournal.net/article/view/3604

Overview on Metoidioplasty: Variants of the Technique. https://doi.org/10.1038/s41443-020-00346-y

Overview of Surgical Techniques in Gender-Affirming Genital Surgery. https://tau.amegroups.com/article/view/26632/24262

The Role of Clitoral Anatomy in Female to Male Sex Reassignment Surgery. www.hindawi.com/journals/tswj/2014/437378/

University of North Carolina School of Medicine Embryo images online. https://syllabus.med.unc.edu/courseware/embryo_images

Vaping 'No Better' than Smoking when Surgery Needed. www.sciencedaily.com/releases/2017/11/171115175653.htm

Why It's Important: Cervical Screening. www.nhs.uk/conditions/cervical-screening/why-its-important

Phalloplasty

Complication of Osteo Reconstruction by Utilizing Free Vascularized Fibular Bone Graft. https://bmcsurg.biomedcentral.com/articles/10.1186/s12893-020-00875-9

Latissimus Dorsi Free Flap Phalloplasty: A Systematic Review. www.nature.com/articles/s41443-020-00371-x

Lovehoney Twin Teasers Textured Penis Sleeves. www.lovehoney.co.uk/sex-toys/male-sex-toys/penis-extenders-sleeves/p/lovehoney-twin-teasers-textured-penis-sleeves-2-pack/a34731g62788.html

Patients' Guide to Phalloplasty Techniques. St Peter's Andrology Centre, London. www.andrology.co.uk/phalloplasty/phalloplasty-resources

Penile Prosthesis. www.andrology.co.uk/phalloplasty/penile-prosthesis

Phalloplasty: A Review of Techniques and Outcomes. https://pubmed.ncbi.nlm.nih.gov/27556603

Phalloplasty for Gender Affirmation. www.hopkinsmedicine.org/center-transgender-health/services-appointments/faq/phalloplasty

Preexpansion in Phalloplasty Patients: Is It Effective? www.semanticscholar.org/paper/Preexpansion-in-Phalloplasty-Patients%3A-Is-It-Elfering-Sluis/791ff2da922eb9dbce4e230313aeb87f0bf2c658

Suprapubic Phalloplasty in Transmen: Surgical Results and Critical Review. https://pubmed.ncbi.nlm.nih.gov/33727691/

Tests and Next Steps: Womb (Uterus) Cancer. www.nhs.uk/conditions/womb-cancer/tests-and-next-steps/

Total Phallic Construction Techniques in Transgender Men: An Updated Narrative Review. https://tau.amegroups.com/article/view/66769/html

Trans Pregnancy: Fertility, Reproduction and Body Autonomy. www.tandfonline.com/doi/full/10.1080/26895269.2021.1884289

Undergoing Tissue Expansion: Chloe's Story. www.youtube.com/watch?v=fzOl8o_1dzM&ab_channel=NationwideChildrens

Vaginoplasty, Vulvoplasty and Orchiectomy

Gender Affirming Surgery: Considerations for Vaginoplasty. www.youtube.com/watch?v=lwEu_iwNCq0&t=1119s&ab_channel=UCLAHealth

How Does Tucking Work and Is It Safe? www.healthline.com/health/transgender/tucking

Introduction to Vaginal Dilation after Vaginoplasty. www.youtube.com/watch?v=US7Lr0gVFIA&ab_channel=JohnsHopkinsMedicine

Instagram Live Q&A – Gender Confirmation Surgery with Mr Inglefield. www.youtube.com/watch?v=G5jpmfSzWDI&ab_channel=TheLondonTransgenderClinic

Neovaginal Construction with Pelvic Peritoneum: Reviewing an Old Approach for a New Application. https://doi.org/10.1002/ca.23019

Orchiectomy in Transgender Individuals: A Motivation Analysis and Report of Surgical Outcomes. www.tandfonline.com/doi/full/10.1080/26895269.2020.1749921

Outcome of Vaginoplasty in Male-to-Female Transgenders: A Systematic Review of Surgical Techniques. www.jsm.jsexmed.org/article/S1743-6095(15)31059-6/fulltext

Supporting Sexuality and Improving Sexual Function in Transgender Persons. www.nature.com/articles/s41585-018-0108-8

The Labia Library. www.thelabialibrary.org.au

The Vulva Gallery. thevulvagallery.com

This Womb Transplant Breakthrough Could Open Up Pregnancy to All Sexes. www.theguardian.com/commentisfree/2018/dec/06/live-birth-dead-donor-definition-motherhood-transplants-pregnancy

Transgender Vaginoplasty: Techniques and Outcomes. https://tau.amegroups.com/article/view/26287/24263

Uterine Transplantation and Donation in Transgender Individuals: Proof of Concept. www.tandfonline.com/doi/full/10.1080/26895269.2021.1915635

What's Tucking? How Do I Tuck? https://sexted.org/faq/whats-tucking-how-do-i-tuck

With Womb Transplants a Reality, Transgender Women Dare to Dream of Pregnancies. www.statnews.com/2016/03/07/uterine-transplant-transgender/

Your Sex Life and Testicular Cancer. www.cancerresearchuk.org/about-cancer/testicular-cancer/living-with/sexlife

Zero Depth Vaginoplasty (ZDV). https://marcibowers.com/transfem/zero-depth-vaginoplasty-zdv

Vocal Surgery

How Is Voice Produced? www.swedish.org/services/swedish-otolaryngology/our-services/voice-and-swallowing-disorders-center/how-is-voice-produced

The Voice Foundation: Advancing Understanding of the Voice through Interdisciplinary Research & Education. https://voicefoundation.org/health-science/voice-disorders/anatomy-physiology-of-voice-production/understanding-voice-production

Transgender Voice or Voice Feminization. www.thespeechnetwork.co.uk/transgender

Vocal Effects: How Hormones Change the Way We Sound. https://lithub.com/vocal-effects-how-hormones-change-the-way-we-sound

Vocal Feminization for Transgender Women: Current Strategies and Patient Perspectives. www.dovepress.com/vocal-feminization-for-transgender-women-current-strategies-and-patien-peer-reviewed-fulltext-article-IJGM

Voice Deepening Surgery. www.kursatyelken.co.uk/voice-deepening

Voice Masculinization. https://professionalvoice.org/masculinization.aspx

Preparing for Surgery

Before Surgery. www.nhs.uk/conditions/having-surgery/preparation

DVT (Deep Vein Thrombosis). www.nhs.uk/conditions/deep-vein-thrombosis-dvt

Genital Gender Affirming Surgery: Masculinizing Surgery with Metoidioplasty. www.youtube.com/watch?v=uA5iYrOzVyw&ab_channel=UCLAHealth

Obesity. www.asahq.org/madeforthismoment/preparing-for-surgery/risks/obesity

Quit Smoking. www.nhs.uk/better-health/quit-smoking

Fertility, Contraception and Having a Baby

Bouman, W.P. (2017). *Transgender Handbook: A Guide for Transgender People, Their Families & Professionals*. New York: Nova Science Publishers, Inc. Chapter 2.

Condoms. www.tht.org.uk/hiv-and-sexual-health/sexual-health/improving-your-sexual-health/condoms

Contraception across Transgender. www.nature.com/articles/s41443-021-00412-z

Embryo Cryopreservation. https://mft.nhs.uk/saint-marys/services/gynaecology/reproductive-medicine/embryo-freezing

Ovarian Follicle. www.cancer.gov/publications/dictionaries/cancer-terms/def/ovarian-follicle

Scars

How to Treat Scars on Black Skin. www.medicalnewstoday.com/articles/scars-on-black-skin

Keloid Scars. www.nhs.uk/conditions/keloid-scars
Scar Information: Caring for Your Scar. www.hey.nhs.uk/patient-leaflet/
   scar-information
Shade, Clothing, and Sunscreen. www.aad.org/public/everyday-care/sun-
   protection/shade-clothing-sunscreen
Treatment. www.nhs.uk/conditions/scars/treatment

Sex

List of LGBTQ+ Terms. www.stonewall.org.uk/list-lgbtq-terms
Sex Toys for Trans Pleasure: An Introduction. https://sexted.org/faq/sex-toys-
   for-trans-pleasure-an-introduction-2
Sexual Experiences in Transgender People: The Role of Desire for Gender-
   Confirming Interventions, Psychological Well-Being, and Body Satisfaction.
   www.tandfonline.com/doi/full/10.1080/0092623X.2017.1405303
Sexual Orientation in Transgender Individuals: Results from the Longitudinal
   ENIGI Study. www.nature.com/articles/s41443-020-00402-7

Sexual Health and Check-Ups

An Approach to Discussing Personal and Social Identity Terminology with
   Patients. https://pubmed.ncbi.nlm.nih.gov/29178466
Fallopian Tube Cancer. www.cancerresearchuk.org/about-cancer/ovarian-
   cancer/types/epithelial-ovarian-cancers/fallopian-tube
Overview: Vulvar Cancer. www.nhs.uk/conditions/vulval-cancer
Prostate Cancer Prevention – Patient Version. www.cancer.gov/types/prostate/
   patient/prostate-prevention-pdq
Prostate Problems. www.nhs.uk/conditions/prostate-problems
Safe Sex for Transgender People. https://onlinedoctor.lloydspharmacy.com/uk/
   sexual-health-advice/safe-sex-for-transgender-people

General Sources

Evaluation of BMI as a Risk Factor for Complications following Gender-
   Affirming Penile Inversion Vaginoplasty. https://pubmed.ncbi.nlm.nih.
   gov/31044103/
ICD-11 for Mortality and Morbidity Statistics. https://icd.who.int/browse11/l-m/
   en
NHS England Gender Identity Services for Adults (Non-Surgical Interventions).
   www.england.nhs.uk/publication/service-specification-gender-identity-
   services-for-adults-non-surgical-interventions
NHS England Gender Identity Services for Adults (Surgical Interventions).
   www.england.nhs.uk/publication/service-specification-gender-identity-
   services-for-adults-surgical-interventions
Oxford University Hospitals (2015). Anaesthetic Risks if You Have a High Body
   Mass Index (BMI) Information for Patients. Oxford: Oxford University
   Hospitals. www.ouh.nhs.uk/services/departments/anaesthetics/leaflets.aspx
Review of the Transgender Literature: Where Do We Go from Here? https://
   pubmed.ncbi.nlm.nih.gov/29082332
The Adult Trans Care Pathway. www.cqc.org.uk/guidance-providers/healthcare/
   adult-trans-care-pathway

Further Resources

There are a lot of websites out there now, some run by organisations, some by activists and bloggers, all with resource lists for further information. It is fantastic to see, but also can be a bit overwhelming. So I've kept this list quite short. This list focuses on websites that have specific information about surgery, bodies, fertility, parenting or sexual health in greater detail than I could cover here.

GLAAD
Big collection of resources for transgender people in the USA.
www.glaad.org/transgender/resources

LGBT consortium
A consortium of grassroots LGBT organisations in the UK, useful for searching for local support.
www.consortium.lgbt

Metoidioplasty.net
A website dedicated to providing information about metoidioplasty.
www.metoidioplasty.net

MTFsurgery.net
A website dedicated to providing information on surgery options for transfeminine and non-binary AMAB people.
www.mtfsurgery.net

National Center for Transgender Equality
National organisation in USA advocating for transgender equality.
https://transequality.org

Oh Joy Sex Toy
Online sex positive comic.
www.ohjoysextoy.com

Phallo.net
A website dedicated to providing information about phalloplasty.
www.phallo.net

Pride & Joy BBC podcast
A podcast from the BBC on queer people having children, including stories from trans parents.
www.bbc.co.uk/programmes/p08cklsr/episodes/player

Seahorse documentary
Documentary about a trans man's experience of starting his own family.
https://seahorsefilm.com

Sex Siopa
Online sex toy boutique, offering a personalised service to help trans and non-binary people find the right toy to suit them.
https://sexsiopa.ie

Terrence Higgins Trust
UK-based sexual health charity with dedicated pages for trans and non-binary people.
www.tht.org.uk/hiv-and-sexual-health/sexual-health/trans-people

The Labia Library
The Labia Library is a website about showing that, just like any other part of the body, labia come in all shapes and sizes.
www.labialibrary.org.au

The Penis Gallery

A collection of photos of penises, to show the range of sizes and shapes.

www.thebookofman.com/mind/masculinity/the-penis-gallery

The Vulva Gallery

The Vulva Gallery is an educational platform centred around illustrated vulva portraits and personal stories.

www.thevulvagallery.com

Trans Bucket

A collection of photos of gender confirmation surgery results for trans and non-binary people, created by trans and non-binary people.

Transbucket.com

Transgender Care Listings

A list of trans care providers in the USA.

www.transcaresite.org

Trans-Parenting

USA-based website dedicated to supporting trans parents.

www.trans-parenting.com

WPATH Version 8

The latest worldwide standards of care for trans people.

www.wpath.org/soc8

Index

Subheadings in *italics* indicate tables and figures.

Notes

. . . .
. . . .
. . . .
. . . .
. . . .
. . . .
. . . .
. . . .
. . . .
. . . .
. . . .
. . . .
. . . .
. . . .
. . . .
. . . .
. . . .